The Global Historical and Contemporary Impacts of Voluntary Membership Associations on Human Societies

Voluntaristics Review

Editor-in-Chief

David Horton Smith (*Boston College, USA*)

Associate Editors

Samir Abu-Rumman (*Gulf Opinions Center for Polls and Statistics, Kuwait / Jordan*)
Abdullah Al-Khalifa (*National Center for Social Studies, Saudi Arabia*)
Aries Arugay (*University of the Philippines at Dilliman, Philippines*)
Doug Baer (*University of Victoria, Canada*)
René Bekkers (*VU University Amsterdam, Netherlands*)
Oonagh B. Breen (*University College Dublin, Ireland*)
Grace Chikoto (*University of Wisconsin-Milwaukee, USA*)
Vincent Chua (*National University of Singapore, Singapore*)
Ram A. Cnaan (*University of Pennsylvania, USA / Israel*)
Carolyn Cordery (*Victoria University of Wellington, New Zealand, & Aston University, UK*)
Noshir Dadrawala (*Centre for Advancement of Philanthropy, India*)
Bronwen Dalton (*University of Technology Sydney, Australia*)
Thomas Davies (*City, University of London, UK*)
Justin Davis-Smith (*City, University of London, UK*)
Angela Ellis-Paine (*University of Birmingham, UK*)
Sherine El-Taraboulsi (*University of Oxford, UK / Egypt*)
Chao Guo (*University of Pennsylvania, USA / China*)
Adam Habib (*University of the Witwatersrand, South Africa*)
Mark Hager (*Arizona State University, USA*)
Debbie Haski-Leventhal (*Macquarie University, Australia*) (*Israel*)
Steinunn Hrafnsdottir (*University of Iceland, Iceland*)
Lev Jakobson (*National Research University Higher School of Economics, Russian Federation*)
Emma Juaneda-Ayensa (*La Rioja University, Spain*)
Chulhee Kang (*Yonsei University, South Korea*)
Helena Kuvikova (*Matej Bel University, Slovakia*)
Benjamin Lough (*University of Illinois, USA*)
Jacob Mwathi Mati (*University of the South Pacific at Laucala, Fiji / Kenya*)
Myles McGregor-Lowndes (*Queensland University of Technology, Australia*)
John McNutt (*University of Delaware, USA*)

Irina Mersianova (*National Research University Higher School of Economics, Russian Federation*)
Carl Milofsky (*Bucknell University, USA*)
Alisa Moldavanova (*Wayne State University, USA / Ukraine*)
Andrew Morris (*Union College, USA*)
Bhekinkosi Moyo (*Southern Africa Trust, South Africa*)
Hanna Nel (*University of Johannesburg, South Africa*)
Rebecca Nesbit (*University of Georgia, USA*)
Ebenezer Obadare (*University of Kansas, USA / Nigeria*)
Tomofumi Oka (*Sophia University, Japan*)
Aya Okada (*Kanazawa University, Japan*)
Jennie Onyx (*University of Technology Sydney, Australia*)
Anne B. Pessi (*University of Helsinki, Finland*)
Ruman Petrov (*New Bulgarian University, Bulgaria*)
Cristian Pliscoff (*University of Chile, Chile*)
Tereza Pospisilova (*Charles University, Czech Republic*)
Lionel Prouteau (*Université de Nantes, France*)
Jack Quarter (*University of Toronto, Canada*)
Colin Rochester (*Birkbeck University, UK*)
Krishna Roka (*University of Wisconsin-Stevens Point, USA / Nepal*)
Boguslawa Sardinha (*Instituto Politécnico de Setúbal, Portugal*)
Gregory D. Saxton (*SUNY, University of Buffalo, USA*)
Per Selle (*University of Bergen, Norway*)
Robert A. Stebbins (*University of Calgary, Canada / USA*)
Richard Steinberg (*Indiana University-Purdue University at Indianapolis, USA*)
Hironori Tarumi (*Hokkai-Gakuen University, Japan*)
Marilyn Taylor (*University of the West of England, UK*)
Lars Torpe (*Aalborg University, Denmark*)
Stijn Van Puyvelde (*Vrije Universiteit Brussel, Belgium*)
Jon Van Til (*Rutgers University-Camden, USA*)
Lili Wang (*Arizona State University, USA / China*)
Ming Wang (*Tsinghua University, China*)
Pamala Wiepking (*Erasmus University, Netherlands*)
Fengshi Wu (*Nanyang Technological University, Singapore / China*)
Ruijun Yuan (*Peking University, China*)
Zhibin Zhang (*Flinders University, Australia / China*)
Jiangang Zhu (*Sun Yat-sen University, China*)
Annette Zimmer (*University of Münster, Germany*)

Volumes published in this Brill Research Perspectives title are listed at *brill.com/vrbr*

The Global Historical and Contemporary Impacts of Voluntary Membership Associations on Human Societies

A Literature Review

By

David Horton Smith

BRILL

LEIDEN | BOSTON

This paperback book edition is simultaneously published as issue 2.5–6 (2017) of *Voluntaristics Review*, DOI 10.1163/24054933-12340019.

ICSERA is a global infrastructure organization, research-information institute, and umbrella association for voluntaristics (nonprofit, third sector) researcher associations (www.icsera.org). A Florida-based, IRS-501(c) (3) nonprofit 2010+, the International Council of Voluntarism, Civil Society, and Social Economy Researcher Associations officially sponsors *Voluntaristics Review* and the *Palgrave Handbook of Volunteering, Civic Participation, and Nonprofit Associations.*

Support from the Basic Research Program of the National Research University Higher School of Economics in Moscow, Russian Federation, is gratefully acknowledged.

Library of Congress Control Number: 2018939380

Typeface for the Latin, Greek, and Cyrillic scripts: "Brill". See and download: brill.com/brill-typeface.

ISBN 978-90-04-37188-0 (paperback)
ISBN 978-90-04-37189-7 (e-book)

Copyright 2018 by David Horton Smith.
Published by Koninklijke Brill NV, Leiden, The Netherlands.
Koninklijke Brill NV incorporates the imprints Brill, Brill Hes & De Graaf, Brill Nijhoff, Brill Rodopi,
Brill Sense and Hotei Publishing.
Koninklijke Brill NV reserves the right to protect the publication against unauthorized use and to authorize dissemination by means of offprints, legitimate photocopies, microform editions, reprints, translations, and secondary information sources, such as abstracting and indexing services including databases. Requests for commercial re-use, use of parts of the publication, and/or translations must be addressed to Koninklijke Brill NV.

This book is printed on acid-free paper and produced in a sustainable manner.

Contents

Editorial Introduction: The Beat of a Different Drum—Voluntary
Associations as an Alternative and Neglected Voluntary Sector
Paradigm   XI
     Colin Rochester
Author Biography   XIV

The Global Historical and Contemporary Impacts of Voluntary
Membership Associations on Human Societies: A Literature Review   1
     David Horton Smith

  Abstract   1
  Keywords   2
  Synopsis   2
  A   Overview   4
  B   Definitions   10
     1   *Association*   10
     2   *Effectiveness of Nonprofit Groups*   10
     3   *Efficiency of Nonprofit Groups*   11
     4   *Impact of a Nonprofit Group/the VNPS*   11
     5   *Inputs to Nonprofit Groups*   11
     6   *Membership Association (MA)*   11
     7   *Nonprofit Agency (NPA; or Voluntary Agency; Volag)*   11
     8   *Nonprofit Association*   12
     9   *Nonprofit Organization (NPO; or Nongovernmental Organization/
          NGO)*   12
     10   *Nonprofit Sector (NPS), or Voluntary Nonprofit Sector (VNPS)*   12
     11   *Outcomes of Nonprofit Groups/the VNPS*   13
     12   *Outputs of Nonprofit Groups/the VNPS*   13
     13   *Social Movement (SM)*   14
     14   *Social Movement Group (SMG)*   14
     15   *Social Movement Organization (SMO)*   14
     16   *Stakeholder*   14
     17   *Volag (Voluntary Agency)*   15
     18   *Voluntary Nonprofit Sector (VNPS)*   15
     19   *Voluntaristics*   15

VIII
CONTENTS

C Scientific Paradigm Shifts, Metaphors, and Broader Meanings of Global Impact 16

    1 *Astrophysical Dark Matter Metaphor* 16

    2 *Flat-Earth Maps Metaphor* 17

    3 *Global Animal/Plant Importance Metaphor* 17

    4 *Global Nonprofit Organizations Impact Metaphor* 18

    5 *Metaphor of Global VNPS Origins of Nearly All Government Functions Services* 18

    6 *Metaphor of Global Importance of Paid Work Activity and Work Organizations versus Global Importance of Leisure/Play Activity and Leisure MAs for a High Quality of Life and Felt Happiness* 19

    7 *Metaphor that in Addition to Felt Satisfactions and Happiness being Higher on Average for People Affiliated with MAs as Volunteers than for People Affiliated with Volags as Paid Staff, MAs on Average Command More Commitment from Participants than Do Volags* 20

D Historical Background of MA Impact Research 20

E Key Association Types for Global Impact 24

    1 *Revolutionary, Guerrilla, and Civil War MAS* 25

    2 *Underground Political Resistance MAs in Foreign-Army-Occupied Nations/Societies* 27

    3 *Terrorist MAS* 30

    4 *Hate Groups as MAS* 31

    5 *Deviant Voluntary Associations in General as MAS* 32

    6 *Social Movements and Social Movement Organizations (SMOs) as MAS* 35

    7 *Political Interest Groups or Pressure Groups as MAS* 41

    8 *Political Parties as MAS* 44

    9 *Democratization MAS* 47

    10 *Religious MAs and Movements* 51

        (a) The Dark Side of Religion 55

    11 *Scientific-Learned MAS* 56

    12 *Economic-Support MAS* 58

        (a) Trade and Business MAS/TBAS 58

        (b) Trade/Labor Union MAS 58

        (c) Farmers' MAS 59

        (d) Professional MAS 59

CONTENTS IX

13 *Social Innovation and Sustainable Development MAS*   60
    (a) Four Global Associational Revolutions in Human History Affecting SD   61
    (b) Key Social Innovations Fostering SD in Global Associational History   63
    (c) Global Impacts of Associations Affecting SD   65
    (d) Associations and Volunteering as Public Participation in SD   65
14 *List/Typology of Major MA Purpose/Goal Subtypes*   67

F Conclusion   68
    1 *Some of My Prior Relevant Conclusions about MAS*   68
    2 *Several New Conclusions about MAS from This Review Paper*   70
    3 *Basic Thesis of This Paper*   77
    4 *Smith's Prior Round-Earth Map/Approach for VNPS Study (Smith, 2000, pp. 217–242, Chap. 10)*   79

G Recent Trends and Research Needed   81

H Usable Knowledge   82
    1 *Summary of the Research Reviewed*   82
    2 *The Need for a Paradigm Shift in Voluntaristics/Nonprofits Research Regarding MAS/NMAS*   82

I Bibliography   83

Editorial Introduction: The Beat of a Different Drum—Voluntary Associations as an Alternative and Neglected Voluntary Sector Paradigm

In his latest major contribution to the study of voluntary associations, David Horton Smith makes a friendly reference to a book I published recently. In *Rediscovering voluntary action: The beat of a different drum* (Palgrave Macmillan, 2013), I challenged the conventional view of the nature of the UK's voluntary sector and, by implication, of the nonprofit sector in the US and elsewhere. I argued that we needed a fresh approach and "the development of an alternative paradigm."

During the forty-five-plus years of my involvement in the practice and study of voluntary action, I have witnessed a growing concentration of interest in a narrow spectrum of voluntary *agencies* (nearly always operated mainly by paid staff) to the exclusion of the wider number of groups and organizations, mainly voluntary *associations*. Such membership associations, most of them local in scope and operated solely by volunteers, have most clearly exemplified the distinctive characteristics of, and the contribution to society made by, the voluntary sector. For many decades, the scholarly and also general public view of the voluntary sector has been dominated by the purposes and methods of the comparatively small number of professionally staffed, bureaucratically organized, and managerially focused agencies that have increasingly reflected the concerns of government and also have adopted the methods of the private for-profit sector. As a result, most of the values, aims, and practices of the much greater number of the voluntary associations (together with some ambiguous voluntary agencies that combine the world of the association with the workings of bureaucracies) have been largely written out of the story.

Rediscovering voluntary action argues for "a realignment of our map of the voluntary sector or ... a shift in the sector's centre of gravity." Instead of concentrating on the largest and most bureaucratic forms of voluntary organization, my "alternative paradigm focuses attention on the organisational forms that exhibit the organisational features that define the distinctive nature of voluntary action." The book also sets out a research agenda that will "concentrate on the activities and behaviour of *unmanaged volunteers involved in non-bureaucratic organisational settings*." The aims of such an agenda would be to identify the ways in which voluntary action is different from other forms of collective activity and how non-bureaucratic voluntary groups are organised and managed in special ways.

These aspirations echo some of the concerns that have shaped the long and fertile intellectual journey undertaken by David Horton Smith over more than fifty years, during which he has published a series of influential articles and several major books promoting voluntary action and explaining the importance within it of the role of membership associations. He has developed two striking metaphors that characterized associations as the *dark matter* of the voluntary nonprofit sector and has explained the lack of scholarly interest in them by reference to the prevalence of *flat earth maps* of the sector's territory. His magisterial survey of *Grassroots associations* (SAGE, 2000) provided a comprehensive account of the behavior of these organizations and the recent publication of *The Palgrave handbook of volunteering, civic participation, and nonprofit associations* (Palgrave Macmillan, 2016), which he co-edited with Bob Stebbins and Jurgen Grotz, has provided an encyclopedic account of voluntary action on a global scale, especially volunteering and membership associations.

And not least of his contributions to the study of voluntary action has been the development of an emerging academic discipline that reflects his wide-ranging concerns (and has been enshrined in the title of this journal). I have to admit that I find the name he has chosen—*Voluntaristics*—far from euphonious, but I have no concerns about the utility of the term that embraces a wide range of "individual and collective human phenomena ... that involve relatively non-coerced, free will decisions and behaviors" and which, as well as broadening the focus of these activities, distances them from what now increasingly seems to be the discredited, or at least often ignored, concept of voluntary action.

David Horton Smith's latest contribution to the study of voluntaristics in this issue of *Voluntaristics Review*, Vol. 2, No. 5–6, is typically ambitious in its scope. It seeks to demonstrate just how important membership associations are to the historical development of human society and sets out his stall in a broad-brush approach and painting a broad canvas. In the first place, he draws on evidence from an historical account that goes back for 300 years. Secondly, he reviews experience collected from a range of geographical sources; while much of his evidence is based on the US and Western Europe, he also presents significant examples of experience drawn from Latin America, Asia, and Africa. The third dimension of the scope of his interests sets out the variety of issues or topics covered by his review, including some general features of voluntary associations that contribute to their important historical impacts since the Industrial Revolution.

Much of the material he covers could be described in broad terms as political: he reviews the impact on the historical development of society from the perspective of associations that promote social change through various kinds

EDITORIAL INTRODUCTION

of political activity. These have been involved in social movements and social movement organizations; associations that promote revolutions, guerrilla activities, and civil wars; associations that promote democracy; underground resistance movements and other *deviant* groups; single-issue interest and pressure groups; and the role of political parties as membership associations. While many of these organizations may individually have limited impact on social and political change, their cumulative or aggregated effects are, as Smith argues, profound. He also calls to mind other kinds of membership association which play their parts in our wider society—those who organize around shared religious beliefs; those which support businesses, farmers, factory workers, or specific professions; and a variety of other kinds of purposes for which associations organize and provide support.

The variety of associational forms brought together in this article and the range of literature on which it is based inevitably produce an account which is wide-ranging but can be criticized as lacking detail. Arguably, each one of Smith's types of association and its impact on society requires not just an article but quite possibly a book to support his overall contention that they demonstrate just how important membership associations are to the historical development of human society (although he cites many such relevant books in each section). Such criticism would be to mistake what I would see as the main purpose of the current article. What Smith has done—as he has often done before—is to shine the strong beam of his wide-angled searchlight on his perceptions about the importance of membership associations in such a way that no-one can ignore what he has to say about them. Clearly, such associations have had major impacts on societies and history in the past two and a half centuries—likely more impact than most academics, let alone the general public, have understood or recognized.

Colin Rochester
Visiting Senior Fellow
The London School of Economics and Political Science, London, UK

Author Biography

David Horton Smith

Smith is Research and Emeritus Professor of Sociology, Boston College, USA; Honorary Visiting Professor, Centre for Studies of Civil Society and the Nonprofit Sector, National Research University Higher School of Economics, Moscow, Russia; Honorary Visiting Professor, School of Arts and Sciences, City, University of London, London, UK; Visiting Scholar, Flinders University, Adelaide, Australia; Visiting Scholar, Institute for Philanthropy, Tsinghua University, Beijing, China.

David's Sociology Ph.D. is from Harvard University (1965). He founded (1971) the global Association for Research on Nonprofit Organizations and Voluntary Action/ ARNOVA (www.arnova.org) and the *Nonprofit and Voluntary Sector Quarterly/NVSQ*, an SSCI journal. David won the ARNOVA Lifetime Achievement Award for Distinguished Contribution to Nonprofit and Voluntary Action Research in 1993, the first time awarded. He co-received the 1975 national Hadley Cantril Memorial Award for the outstanding U.S. behavioral and social sciences book. He founded (2010) and leads ICSERA, the International Council of Voluntarism, Civil Society, and Social Economy Researcher Associations (www.icsera.org), a global, nonprofit sector, infrastructure organization. He founded the *Voluntaristics Review: Brill Research Perspectives,* a journal of lengthy survey/review articles (Brill, 2016–).

David is author of *Grassroots Associations* (Sage, 2000), first co-author of *A Dictionary of Nonprofit Terms and Concepts* (Indiana University Press, 2006), second co-author of the *2011 State of the World's Volunteerism Report* (UN Volunteers, 2011), and the first Co-Editor and principal author of the *Palgrave Handbook of Volunteering, Civic Participation, and Nonprofit Associations* (Palgrave Macmillan, 2016). His latest book is *S-Theory (Synanthrometrics) As A Theory of Everyone: A Proposed New Standard Human Science Model of Behavior, Especially Pro-Social Behavior* (under editorial review). He is author/editor of 13 other books, and over 100 journal articles. His bio has been in Marquis' *Who's Who in the World* since 2001, and he won the Albert Nelson Marquis Lifetime Achievement Award from Marquis' Who's Who. His bio is among 139 in *International Encyclopedia of Civil Society* (Springer, 2010) as outstanding nonprofit sector leaders and researchers from all nations and history.

The Global Historical and Contemporary Impacts of Voluntary Membership Associations on Human Societies
A Literature Review

David Horton Smith*

Ph.D., Research and Emeritus Professor, Department of Sociology, Boston College, Chestnut Hill, USA

Honorary Visiting Research Professor, Centre for Studies of Civil Society and the Nonprofit Sector, National Research University Higher School of Economics, Moscow, Russian Federation

Honorary Visiting Professor, School of Arts and Sciences, City, University of London, London, UK

Visiting Scholar, Institute for Philanthropy, Tsinghua University, Beijing, China

Honorary Visiting Scholar, Australian Center for Community Studies and Research, Flinders University, Adelaide, Australia

dhortonsmith@hotmail.com

Abstract

Reviewed here is global research on how 13 types of Voluntary Membership Associations (MAS) have significantly or substantially had global impacts on human history, societies, and life. Such outcomes have occurred especially in the past 200+ years since the Industrial Revolution circa 1800 CE, and its accompanying Organizational Revolution. Emphasized are longer-term, historical, and societal or multinational impacts of MAS, rather than more micro-level (individual) or meso-level (organizational) outcomes. MAS are distinctively structured, with power coming from the membership, not top-down. The author has characterized MAS as the *dark matter* of the nonprofit/third sector, using an astrophysical metaphor. Astrophysicists have shown that *most* physical matter in the universe is dark in the sense of being unseen, not stars or planets.

---

* The author is grateful to the following colleagues for helpful comments on prior drafts of this article: Christopher Corbett; John McNutt; Carl Milofsky; and Colin Rochester.

Keywords

voluntary associations – impact of associations – global historical impact of associations – nonprofit associations – membership associations – common interest associations – association effectiveness – association outcomes – nonprofit organizations/NPOS – nongovernmental organizations/NGOS – voluntary nonprofit sector – voluntaristics research – social movements – political interest groups – deviant voluntary associations

Synopsis

This document reviews the global research literature on how Voluntary Membership Associations (abbreviated as MAS) have significantly, and often substantially, had global impacts on human history, societies, and life, especially in the past 200 or so years since the Industrial Revolution circa 1800 CE, and its accompanying Organizational Revolution (Boulding, 1953). This third organizational revolution was one of four such global associational revolutions identified by Smith (2018d; see also Smith, 1972a). Smith (1997b) has described the 10,000-year history of MAS as the first kind of nonprofit organizations (NPOS) to arise in human societies (see also, Harris et al., 2016). MAS are also the most frequent type of NPOS in all societies ever properly studied or estimated (Smith, 2014c; Smith et al., 2016a; Smith et al., 2016b).

The fundamental thesis of this paper is that MAS have had for centuries and continue to have far more substantial and enduring importance, influence, and impact in contemporary societies worldwide than is commonly recognized, even by most voluntaristics/nonprofit scholars (Smith, 2013, 2016a). Exceptions include especially the wide-ranging and important book by Rochester (2013), entitled *Rediscovering voluntary action: The beat of a different drum* (see also, Rochester et al., 2010). Long ago, Smith (1973b, 1974, 1975), Smith with Dixon (1973), and Smith, Reddy, and Baldwin (1972) edited books and wrote chapters studying and promoting voluntary action, as effortful activity one is "neither made to nor paid to do," with formal volunteering in MAS as his primary concern. C. Smith and Freedman (1972) at about the same time wrote an important literature review book on MAS. More recently, there have been important works on MAS by many scholars, particularly Cnaan and Milofsky (2008) and Smith, Stebbins, and Grotz (2016). The present long paper continues in this scholarly tradition, but emphasizes the longer-term, historical, and societal or multinational/global impacts and influences of MAS, rather than their more micro-level (individual) or meso-level (organizational) results.

In various articles and encyclopedia chapters, Smith (e.g., 1997c) has characterized MAS as the *dark matter* of the voluntary nonprofit sector/VNPS (third sector, voluntary sector, charitable sector, civil society, civil society sector, tax-exempt sector, solidarity economy, social economy, etc.; see Smith, Stebbins, & Dover, 2006, p. 63), using an astrophysical metaphor. Astrophysicists have shown that the vast majority of physical matter in the universe is dark in the sense of being unseen, that is, not stars or planets, etc. (Panek, 2011; Seymour, 2008). Another metaphor that seeks to convey the scholarly neglect of MAS perceived by the author and some others is to refer to *flat-earth maps* of the VNPS (Smith, 2000, pp. 13–15), akin to almost universal perception of the earth as flat until circa 1500 CE (Zerubavel, 1992). Section C discusses some additional metaphors that may help convey this paper's basic thesis about relative academic neglect of MAS.

In recent journal articles and encyclopedia chapters, Smith and others have shown that MAS (both local, national, and transnational) are important features of the VNPS for reasons besides their greater age in human history and their very large numbers, noted above (e.g., Smith, 2000, 2004, 2010a, 2010b, 2015b, 2015c, 2017a, 2017b, 2017c, 2017d, 2018b). Some 13 types of MAS, reviewed here, have had significant, often substantial and enduring (over years and decades, sometimes centuries) impacts on contemporary societies/nations worldwide (Gamson, 1990; Giugni, 1998, 2004; Giugni, McAdam, & Tilly, 1999; Skrentny, 2004; Smith, 2018b; Tilly, 2004, 2007; Uba, 2009). Much research has shown that MAS are very distinctively structured, with power usually coming from the bottom up/the membership, rather than top-down/board of directors and top staff, as in governments, businesses, and nonprofit agencies with paid staff (Smith, 2000, Part II; 2017a). Other documents since 2000 have demonstrated that MAS have a wide variety of important impacts on their members and participants as associational/formal volunteers (e.g., Smith, 1997a; 2016b Wilson et al., 2016).

After an introduction, selected definitions, and some historical background, the present review paper is mainly structured around 13 key types of MAS that have had major impacts on societies and the history of nation-states in the past 200 or so years, especially in modern/industrial and post-modern/post-industrial nations. The term *global impact* and its broader meanings are explained in Section C. These key, higher-impact MA types as nonprofit organizations (NPOS) are the following, in the order discussed and also in rough descending order of their tendency to disrupt society and use violence: (1) revolutionary, guerrilla war, and civil war MAS; (2) underground political resistance MAS in foreign-army-occupied nations/societies; (3) terrorist MAS; (4) hate groups as MAS; (5) deviant voluntary associations in general as

MAS; (6) social movements/social movement organizations (SMOS) as MAS; (7) political interest groups or pressure groups as MAS; (8) political parties as MAS; (9) democratization MAS; (10) religious MAS and movements; (11) scientific-learned MAS; (12) economic-support MAS; and (13) social innovation and sustainable development MAS. In the last sub-section of Section E, a recent general list/typology of major MA goal/purpose subtypes is given.

In conclusion, this paper argues that the global historical and societal impacts of MAS, as the first and still most frequent type of NPO (Smith, 2014c), are by far greater than the long-term impact of any other NPO type in contemporary societies/nations worldwide, such as nonprofit agencies (voluntary agencies, Volags, NPAS), foundations, or social enterprises. MAS that have used disruptive, activist protest approaches have been especially successful since circa 1800, but non-violent approaches have also worked at times since 1900. Social movement MAS have been especially successful since about 1800, particularly when they have been involved in the global human rights/minority rights revolution (Skrentny, 2004).

The author further argues (Sections C and H) for a systematic paradigm shift (Kuhn, 1962) in thinking and theory among voluntaristics/nonprofit scholars/academics (Smith, 2016a) who study nonprofits/NPOS and the voluntary nonprofit sector/VNPS (third sector; civil society). The shift I call for requires MAS to be studied more carefully and fully, using a round-earth paradigm (Smith, 2000, pp. 217–241; see also Section F., CONCLUSION, Subsection C, of this paper), as integral and important aspects of the VNPS and all NPOS, rather than often ignored as invisible or inconsequential *dark matter* (Smith, 1997a, 1997c). Most people, including voluntaristics scholars/academics, are misled by thinking about MAS in far too narrow terms, as Scouts, Alcoholics Anonymous/AA, school or university clubs, or sports associations. The correct definition of an MA fits far more important types of NPOS, such as the 13 key MA types reviewed here, that have sometimes brought about substantial, or at least significant, changes in specific societies, especially nation-states, since about 1800, and in the global human society as a whole.

A   Overview

Although most people are not aware of it, including many voluntaristics (altruistics, philanthropy, nonprofits/nonprofit sector, civil society/civil society sector, third sector, charitable sector, tax-exempt sector, voluntarism, social economy, solidarity economy) scholars (Smith, 2016a), nonprofit and usually voluntary Membership Associations (MAS) have had an amazing impact on

HISTORICAL IMPACTS OF VOLUNTARY ASSOCIATIONS

human society in the 10 millennia since they first became widespread on earth, as part of the *horticultural revolution* (Harris et al., 2016; Nolan & Lenski, 2006; Smith, 1997b, 2018d;). Although many such outcomes and impacts have been positive, other outcomes have instead been negative and largely harmful to their members and the larger society or world, sometimes hugely so.

This paper reviews the global research literature on how Voluntary Membership Associations (abbreviated as MAS) have significantly, and often substantially, affected human history, societies, and life, especially in the past 200 or so years since the Industrial Revolution starting circa 1800 CE, and its accompanying Organizational Revolution (Boulding, 1953). This third organizational revolution was one of four such global associational revolutions identified by Smith (2018d; see also Smith, 1972a).

The fundamental thesis of this paper is that MAS have had and continue to have far more importance, influence, and global impact in modern societies than is commonly recognized, even by most voluntaristic/nonprofits scholars (Smith, 2013, 2016). Thus, MAS can properly be seen as the most important type of nonprofit organizations/NPOS (or NPGS, as nonprofit groups, more broadly) in terms of long-term global historical and societal impacts worldwide. Exceptions to relative academic neglect of MA historical impacts and importance include especially the wide-ranging and important book by Rochester (2013), entitled *Rediscovering voluntary action: The beat of a different drum* (see also, Rochester et al., 2010). Long ago, Smith (1973b, 1974, 1975), Smith with Dixon (1973), and Smith, Reddy, and Baldwin (1972) edited books and wrote review chapters studying and promoting voluntary action, as effortful activity one is "neither made to nor paid to do," with formal volunteering in MAS as his primary concern. C. Smith and Freedman (1972) at about the same time wrote an important literature review book on MAS. More recently, there have been important works on MAS by many scholars, particularly Cnaan and Milofsky (2008) and Smith, Stebbins, and Grotz (2016). The present long paper continues in this scholarly tradition, but emphasizes the longer-term, global historical and societal or multinational impacts and influences of MAS, rather than their more micro-level (individual) or meso-level (organizational) results.

Smith (1997b) has described the 10,000-year history of MAS as the first kind of NPOS to arise in human societies (see also, Harris et al., 2016). MAS are also the most frequent type of NPOS in all societies ever properly studied or estimated (Smith, 2014c; Smith et al., 2016a; Smith et al., 2016b). MAS were clearly the first kind of NPOS to arise in human history, though they were more accurately nonprofit groups/NPGS, because initially rather informal and hence not clearly *organizations* (as formal groups) at all (Smith, Stebbins, & Dover, 2006, pp. 156–157, 184–185). Small, local, all-volunteer MAS, termed *grassroots associations* (GAS), were the original form of NPGS for thousands of years (Harris et al., 2016; Smith, 1997b, 2000). Supra-local MAS are much more recent in human history. Because of limitations of transportation and communication, national associations mainly began to flourish only in the 19th century, as a result of the Industrial Revolution and technological changes in a variety of Western nations (Smith, Pospíšilová, & Wu, 2016). For similar reasons, international nonprofit organizations (or international NGOS—INGOS) mainly began to flourish in the late 19th century in such nations, but also in many non-Western nations (Davies et al., 2016).

The first of four distinct, global, economic and associational revolutions in human history (Smith, 2018d), this horticultural revolution involved former hunting-gathering bands/tribes settling down into small, semi-permanent villages. Now they mainly raised crops (initially, various grains and/or root vegetables) by simple gardening (*horticulture*) and also raised and ate certain domesticated animals (cows, pigs, chickens), rather than gathering wild plants and hunting wild animals for food (Nolan & Lenski, 2006, Chap. 6). Preliterate, hunting-gathering bands/tribes had been the usual form of societies for all of the prior 200+ millennia of human existence.

In various articles and encyclopedia chapters, Smith (1997c, for instance) has characterized MAS as the *dark matter* of the voluntary nonprofit sector/VNPS (third sector, voluntary sector, charitable sector, civil society, civil society sector, tax-exempt sector, solidarity economy, social economy, etc.; see Smith, Stebbins, & Dover, 2006, p. 63), using an astrophysical metaphor. Astrophysicists have shown that the vast majority of physical matter in the universe is dark in the sense of being unseen, that is, not stars or planets, etc. (Panek, 2011; Seymour, 2008). Another metaphor that seeks to convey the scholarly neglect of MAS perceived by the author and some other scholars is to refer to *flat-earth maps* of the VNPS (Smith, 2000, pp. 13–15), akin to almost universal perception of the earth as flat until circa 1500 CE (Zerubavel, 1992).

In recent journal articles and encyclopedia chapters, Smith and others have shown that MAS (both local, national, and transnational) are important features of the VNPS for reasons besides their greater age in human history and their very large numbers, noted above (e.g., Smith, 2015b, 2017a, 2017c). Much research has shown that MAS are very distinctively structured, with power usually coming from the bottom up/the membership, rather than top-down/board of directors and top staff, as in governments, businesses, and nonprofit agencies with paid staff (Smith, 2000, Part II; 2017a). Other documents since 2000 have documented that MAS have a wide variety of important impacts on their members and participants as associational/formal volunteers (e.g., Smith, 1997a; 2016b; Wilson et al., 2016).

HISTORICAL IMPACTS OF VOLUNTARY ASSOCIATIONS

The basic contention here is that *MAs have had, and continue to have, substantially more historical impact on human societies worldwide than nonprofit agencies/Volags/NPAs with paid staff,* contrary to common beliefs held by most laypeople and even by most voluntaristics/nonprofit scholars. Thus, *MAs can be seen as the most important type of NPOs (NPGs) in terms of long-term, historical and global impacts on human societies, both on individual societies/nation-states and on the emerging global human society.* This conclusion is reinforced by the clear historical fact that MAs have a 10,000-year-plus (up to 25,000 years, in some cases) history in human societies (Smith, 1997b, 2018d). Paid-staff nonprofit agencies (*voluntary agencies, Volags, NPAs*) serving non-members as selected recipients/users/clients or the general public have had a much shorter history, dating back only 2400 years or so (Smith, 2015c, pp. 261–262). Volags have only been frequent and widespread in human societies for the past two centuries, especially in industrial and post-industrial nations (Chambers, 1985; Critchlow & Parker, 1998; Harris & Bridgen, 2007; Katz, 1986; O'Neill, 1989, see sections of most chapters entitled "Historical development;" Smith, 2015c).

According to the author (Smith, 2015c, p. 262), the first Volag in history was probably the museum of Ennigaldi-Nanna, founded *c.* 530 BC by a Babylonian princess in Ur, now Iraq (ibid., p. 262). Other very early Volags were the first hospital at the Temple of Asclepius at Epidaurus in Greece, from *c.* 430 BC (ibid., p. 261), while Plato's Academy in Athens was likely the first proto-college, from *c.* 387 BC (ibid.). There are several other examples of early Volags of various types (ibid.): libraries, monasteries (but not religious congregations, which are usually associations), secondary schools, universities, almshouses, and orphanages. However, Volags have existed in substantial numbers mainly for the past two centuries (Chambers, 1985; Critchlow & Parker, 1998; Harris & Bridgen, 2007; Harris et al., 2016; Katz, 1986; Smith, 1997b; 2015c, p. 262; Soteri-Proctor et al., 2016).

In the space of this paper (as contrasted with a potentially much longer book), the pervasive, substantial, and very long-term, societal and global historical impact of MAs can only be sketched briefly, qualitatively, and rather superficially, given its actual historical and cross-cultural breadth and variety, and also given the severe difficulties of quantitative evaluations of such outcomes and impacts.

When concerned with evaluating the impacts of NPOs, and their accountability, effectiveness, and efficiency, most voluntaristics scholars focus only on nonprofit agencies with paid staff that attempt to help non-members (Smith, 1997a, 1997c, 2000, Chap. 10, 2015c). Their central impact-interest is on services delivered. Such scholars tend to ignore the more numerous and historically far more important MAs that tend to be smaller, poorer, shorter in lifespans, and usually all-volunteer in their leaders and active participants (Smith, 2000, Chap. 2, 2015b; Smith et al., 2016, Chap. 32). For instance, the widely read handbook on nonprofit leadership and management edited by Renz (2010) has three chapters (4, 15, and 16) dealing with nonprofit accountability, outcome assessment, and evaluating effectiveness. Although Chapter 4 mentions membership organizations, none of these chapters pays any significant attention to the special aspects of evaluating the impact or effectiveness of MAS, especially of grassroots (local, all-volunteer) associations (GAS) (Smith, 2000). The latest edition, Renz and Herman (2016), is similar. The chapter by Kearns (2012), from another edited book, deals with accountability in the VNPS; it takes a similar technocratic view of NPO evaluation. The books on NPO performance, accountability, and evaluation by Anheier (2004), Cutt and Murray (2000), Jordan and Van Tuijl (2007), and Saul (2004) have similar limitations, as do all or nearly all more recent books on these topics (Keehley & Abercrombie, 2008; Newcomer, Hatry, & Wholey, 2015; Penna, 2011; Poister, Aristigueta, & Hall, 2014).

GAS tend to be all-volunteer in leaders and members, and to have no long-term, owned/rented building space (Smith, 2000, 2014c). Thus, most GAS need little money to achieve their goals, which are usually emotional-expressive and serve members, rather than being rational-instrumental and serving mainly non-members, as Volags do (Smith 2015b, 2015c). As a result, *evaluation of the effectiveness, outcomes, and impacts of MAS, most of which are GAS, usually requires a more nuanced, qualitative, and humanistic approach.*

The broader *humanistic approach*, favored by the author and some others, emphasizes that the nonprofit aspect of the VNPS refers mainly to the emphasis of NPOS, especially MAS and GAS, and participating individuals, on *humane values that go far beyond mere profit-seeking (or surplus revenue-seeking) and conformity to government laws and rules.*

There are four main sectors of society: the family/household sector, the business/for-profit sector, the government/public sector, and the VNPS (see Smith, Stebbins, & Dover, 2006, pp. 205–206; also, Smith, 1991, 1993). The VNPS is distinctive among these four main sectors of society in seeking mainly *non*-financial/non-monetary goals. But the *nonprofit* aspect of the VNPS is often interpreted narrowly, as meaning *only* that any surplus revenue of an NPO at the end of a fiscal year is not, by definition, a profit, and by law cannot be distributed to NPO owners/investors or managers—the non-distribution constraint (Hansmann, 1980).

But this is a far too legalistic, financial, and technocratic an approach to fully capture the core meaning and values of the VNPS (Rothschild & Milofsky, 2006). The reason why the non-distribution constraint is widely recognized in the legal systems of contemporary nations, and is often associated with income tax-exemption for an NPO, is precisely the non-monetary, humane core values *assumed* to characterize most NPOs (Weisbrod, 1992).

The non-distribution constraint is but one indicator of the underlying humane core values of most NPOs. Moreover, the non-distribution constraint is useless and trivial for the vast majority of all NPOs (NPGS) in the world now (Smith, 2014c) and ever in the past (Smith, 1997b): Most NPOs are GAS, and have only tiny revenues in any given year at any time in the 10,000-year history of GAS as a form of human group (Harris et al., 2016; Smith, 2000; Smith, Never, et al., 2016b; Smith, Stebbins, & Dover, 2006, p. 24: "associational form of organization"; Soteri-Proctor et al., 2016). The humane core values *test* is thus a far better, deeper, and more reliable guide/test regarding the nonprofit aspect or nature of any NPO, whether a Volag or an MA. Rothschild and Milofsky (2006) have also cogently argued this point about the core values of the VNPS.

Although there are many versions of key humane values, Smith (2000, pp. 22–23) suggested and defined a succinct set of seven *humane core* values: civic engagement, sociopolitical innovation, social religiosity, sociability, social esthetics (-enjoyment-recreation), economic system support, and personal social service. The author adds a few other humane values now: *learning-discovery, personal growth/development*, and *community improvement-development-protection* (see Smith, with Stebbins, et al., 2016; Smith, with van Puyvelde, 2016b). MAS, especially GAS, clearly do a better job of implementing the substance of this set of ten humane core values than do Volags/nonprofit agencies/NPAs, in general, especially if one also considers the de-emphasis on the pursuit of money, income, and assets that generally characterizes MAS, and in theory also characterizes the entire VNPS.

In sum, putting a major emphasis, let alone a *sole* emphasis, on financial/ monetary criteria of importance and value is a grave error in trying to understand and evaluate NPOs and the VNPS in general. However, this is especially an error for understanding and evaluating MAS and particularly GAS as NPOs (or NPGS). Many NPOs, particularly Volags/NPAs, clearly need significant, and often substantial, financial resources to survive and be effective. Large, paid-staff-based MAS, especially at the national or international level of geographic scope, *also* need substantial financial resources, but these are exceptions numerically in the realm of MAS. MAS in general, especially GAS, need few financial resources, as noted above. MAS depend mainly on the efforts of committed members and leaders as active volunteers as their main resources.

Where financial resources are crucial for Volags/nonprofit agencies/NPAs, volunteer commitment and effort are the crucial resources for MAS/NMAS. Most voluntaristics scholars who have focused on Volags fail to understand this, especially when viewed cumulatively and historically, leading them to believe erroneously that the lack of financial resources and paid staff of most MAS condemns them to weakness and ineffectiveness. Given these facts about different resource bases, along with marked differences in their power/authority structures (Smith, 2010a, 2010b, 2015b, 2015c), Smith (1991, 1993) long ago suggested that the *MAS/NMAS and Volags/NPAs should be seen more clearly as two distinct sub-sectors of the VNPS, or perhaps even as different sectors of society. This suggestion is even more relevant and accurate now as a view of the socio-cultural reality of the VNPS*, given extensive subsequent research in the past twenty-five years as cited partially here.

B   Definitions

It is important to define briefly the meanings of some key terms of special relevance here. I sometimes use the term *nonprofit groups* (NPGS) below as broader than the term *nonprofit organizations* (NPOS). NPGS include informal groups, such as many GAS, that do not qualify as formal NPOS. (See *Nonprofit organization* below.)

1   *Association*

a relatively formally structured nonprofit group that depends mainly on volunteer members for participation and activity and that primarily seeks member benefits, even if it may also seek some public benefits. This type of association, frequently referred to as a 'voluntary association' (see classic discussion in C. Smith & Freedman, 1972), is the most common nonprofit in the United States (Smith, 2000, pp. 41–42) [and in all societies or nations ever studied carefully]. The term *common interest association* is sometimes used to underscore the twin facts that associations form around the shared interests of members and tend mainly to serve those interests.

> SMITH, STEBBINS, & DOVER, 2006, P. 23 (Associations are sometimes also termed *nonprofit associations* or *membership associations*, as a type of NPO. See Smith, Stebbins, & Grotz, 2016, pp. 1394, 1399).

2   *Effectiveness of Nonprofit Groups*

how well nonprofit groups accomplish the impact they want to bring about [i.e., their goals] using their structure and operations....

> SMITH, STEBBINS, & DOVER, 2006, P. 75

HISTORICAL IMPACTS OF VOLUNTARY ASSOCIATIONS

3   *Efficiency of Nonprofit Groups*

how well [NPGS'] resources [are] used to make for optimal achievement
of [group goals and intended] outcomes.

> SMITH, 2000, P. 196

4   *Impact of a Nonprofit Group/the VNPS*

Briefly, how an NPG or the VNPS has been shown by research to causally change
things for the better or worse or not at all; for an NPG, impact *includes* how well
it has been shown to have achieved its *intended* goals, if at all. But NPG impact
is much broader than this, including also various *unintended or covertly sought
consequences/outcomes* from the standpoint of many types of relevant stakeholders, who have a right to be involved in assessing whether NPG outcomes
have positive, neutral, or negative impacts. In all cases, the valid and reliable
assessment of NPG impact requires solid scientific research on outcomes done
over significant time (at least years) and valid theories of causation in order to
be credible.

5   *Inputs to Nonprofit Groups*

All of the resources that a NPG receives, owns, or controls and can use to
accomplish its goals and other outcomes, including "money, people, plant,
technology, and brand/reputation" (Smith, Stebbins, & Grotz, 2016, p. 992). The
people involved can have one or more of a variety of possible relationships to
the group, as detailed by Smith (1972b), with paid employees, unpaid volunteers or active members, and policy board members being the most common.
Inputs have no necessary relationship to valued outcomes, let alone to any
positive impacts, of NPGs or of the VNPS, and hence are *not* valid indicators of
impact or effectiveness. However, inputs are easy to count or measure and are
often used by NPG leaders as simplistic evidence of supposed impact or effectiveness, especially when genuine evidence of desired outcomes is missing.

6   *Membership Association (MA)*

Term used in this paper to refer to an association or voluntary association. See
Association.

7   *Nonprofit Agency (NPA; or Voluntary Agency; Volag)*

A nonprofit organization that provides a public service or public benefit (non-member benefit). Such agencies have a corporate structure, not
an associational form of organization. Generally speaking, the nonprofit

agency relies mainly on paid staff to accomplish its goals rather than on members, not having any members. However, service program volunteers may also be used to achieve its goals. The term *voluntary agency* is more commonly used, even if for conceptual consistency, *nonprofit agency* is preferred. Both large and small agencies have a board of directors.

SMITH, STEBBINS, & GROTZ, 2016, P. 1400

8   *Nonprofit Association*

Term used in this paper to refer to an association or voluntary association; an NMA. See *Association*.

9   *Nonprofit Organization (NPO; or Nongovernmental Organization/ NGO)*

a nonprofit group that was founded or has achieved the status of being a formal group, and hence is an organization (Smith, 1972). The term *non-profit organization* emphasizes the not-for-profit (in French, *sans but lucrative*) character of organizations in the nonprofit sector by virtue of the *non-distribution constraint*. This broad constraint on nonprofit organizations requires that such organizations not distribute any literal profit (or surplus/excess revenues) to leaders, staff, or members. This term serves poorly as an umbrella word for *all* the groups comprising the nonprofit sector, because it omits semi-formal and informal non-profits, many of which play an important role there (Smith, 1992). However, many scholars are unaware of or ignore this problem of precise terminology, and incorrectly use the term *nonprofit organization* to refer to all kinds of nonprofit groups.

SMITH, STEBBINS, & GROTZ, 2016, PP. 1401–1402 (*Nonprofit group [NPG]* is the proper general term for all kinds of groups in the VNPS—informal, semi-formal, and formalized [organizations].)

10   *Nonprofit Sector (NPS), or Voluntary Nonprofit Sector (VNPS)*

Preferred general term for the analytical sector of society between the market, the state, and the family/household sector. 1. Narrow definition: sum of all types of volunteer altruism, volunteer action, volunteers, and volunteer groups. 2. Broad definition: sum of the four components set out in sense 1 in addition to all types of quasi-volunteer altruism, quasi-volunteer action, quasi-volunteers, and quasi-volunteer groups (Smith, 2000, p. 27). Generally, the nonprofit sector encompasses all aspects of all nonprofit groups in a society, including nonprofit organizations as formal nonprofit groups, in addition to all individual voluntary action found there. Some sort of nonprofit sector has been found in all societies studied so far [that have achieved the complexity of a residential horticultural society or greater; Nolan & Lenski, 2006; Smith, 1997b]. The terms *voluntary sector, independent sector, third sector, civil society sector, tax-exempt sector, not-for-profit sector, the commons, philanthropic sector, charitable sector* and others are generally used synonymously with sense 2, though in case of the last two terms, emphasis is on charitable nonprofits, such as those registered in the United States with the Internal Revenue Service as 501(c)(3). Burlingame (2004, pp. 355–356) presents distinctions among the various near-synonyms for the nonprofit sector. The nonprofit sector is one of the four main sectors of society (or five sectors, in one scheme), and definitely includes *many* groups and organizations *not* listed or registered by the IRS in the USA or by equivalent government registration agencies in other nations.

SMITH, STEBBINS, & GROTZ, 2016, P. 1402

11   *Outcomes of Nonprofit Groups/the VNPS*

Intended and unintended consequences as states/processes for NPGs, the VNPS, their targets of benefits (intended recipients or beneficiaries), their members and volunteers (who may be internal, member beneficiaries/recipients), their local communities, their local biophysical environments, specific nations/territories, global human society, and the larger biophysical world and universe, or parts thereof, *that seem to result* from the existence and/or activities of NPGs or of the VNPS. In narrower terms, outcomes are consequences that have been shown by reliable research to have resulted in significant part for a specific NPG, set of NPGs, or the VNPS more generally, irrespective of the official (*de jure*) or operative (*de facto*) goals as intended outcomes of an NPG or the VNPS (Perrow, 1961).

12   *Outputs of Nonprofit Groups/the VNPS*

Usually, easily observed or measurable/countable activities or aspects of NPGs that are taken as proxies/substitutes for the actual achievement of group outcomes (e.g., number of phone calls to policy makers by members of a political group; number of attendees at group events or meetings; number of recipients of a group's services; amount of money collected for or spent on a group program or activity; number of hours spent by group members on a program or activity). NPG leaders and members often point to outputs when they lack solid evidence of genuine outcomes sought by an NPG or the VNPS.

13 *Social Movement (SM)*

a collectivity, [which,] working from a shared ideology, [tries] over time either to effect change or to maintain the status quo on a particular issue using in a significant way unconventional political voluntary action (protest activities). In time, the collectivity may coalesce into one or more nonprofit groups (Lofland, 1996). In turn, some of these social movement groups may eventually become formal nonprofit organizations, as in the environmental movement in America (Dunlap & Mertig, 1992) and Western Europe (Dalton, 1994, Part 3).

SMITH, STEBBINS, & DOVER, 2006, P. 213

14 *Social Movement Group (SMG)*

a nonprofit group that is usually a small, often independent, unit in a larger social movement. Based on a shared ideology and common goals but not usually a common bureaucratic structure or even formal affiliation with the larger movement, an SMG tries to effect change (or maintain the status quo, in anti-movements) on a particular issue. The SMG is actually a subtype of political nonprofit. Sometimes incorrectly referred to *as social movement organizations,* most SMGs are informal or semiformal groups [hence not formal organizations at all].

SMITH, STEBBINS, & GROTZ, 2016, P. 1407

15 *Social Movement Organization (SMO)*

a nonprofit social movement group that is formally organized. SMOs are usually associations, not non-profit agencies.

SMITH, STEBBINS, & GROTZ, 2016, P. 1407

16 *Stakeholder*

person, group, organization who can make a [legitimate] claim on a nonprofit group's attention, resources, or output [or outcomes], or who is affected by [these outputs or outcomes].

SMITH, STEBBINS, & DOVER, 2006, P. 219. Usually, there are multiple stakeholders for any NPG, especially when there is any paid staff, which introduces a stake in paid staff remuneration, keeping one's job, and careers for the paid staff, unlike when there are only NPG volunteers, as in all-volunteer associations.

HISTORICAL IMPACTS OF VOLUNTARY ASSOCIATIONS

17   *Volag* (*Voluntary Agency*)

A nonprofit agency, as defined above; an NPA.

18   *Voluntary Nonprofit Sector* (*VNPS*)

See *Nonprofit sector* above, and in Smith, Stebbins, & Dover (2006, p. 159).

19   *Voluntaristics*

The object of study of the emerging academic discipline of voluntaristics is the range of individual and collective human phenomena at various levels of analysis that involve relatively non-coerced, free-will decisions and behaviors, based on values and belief systems which usually involve some aspects of altruism, morality, or other higher (i.e. non-financial) values in the eyes of the participants, whether groups or individuals (see Rothschild & Milofsky, 2006). Voluntaristics phenomena mainly involve normative-voluntary compliance structures, not mainly remunerative or coercive compliance structures, using terminology of Etzioni (1975).

QUOTED WITH PERMISSION FROM SMITH, STEBBINS, & GROTZ, 2016, PP. 1376–1377

Hence, voluntaristics examines those aspects of any society which usually are relatively distinct (a) from families/households, where kinship and close personal relationships dominate exchanges and activities, and communal sharing is the norm; (b) from the market system of exchanges, where market pricing of scarce resources is the norm (business and commercial activities seeking to maximize profits and financial resources), and (c) from the coercive system of exchanges and activities that characterize governments at all territorial levels, where the physical control/ dominance of government and government representatives, agencies, and laws/rules control events and activities (Etzioni, 1975; Smith, 2000, pp. 15–32; Smith, Reddy, & Baldwin, 1972a; Smith, Stebbins, & Dover, 2006, pp. 159, 237–239; Wolfenden Committee, 1978, pp. 22–26). Levels of analysis in voluntaristics range from whole societies, to major segments/sectors of society, to groups and organizations, down to individual motives/dispositions, affects/emotions, goals/outcomes, intellectual abilities, cognitions, the self, [examined both explicitly/consciously and implicitly/unconsciously] and resulting behaviors.

QUOTED WITH PERMISSION FROM SMITH, STEBBINS, & GROTZ, 2016, PP. 1376–1377

16   SMITH

C   **Scientific Paradigm Shifts, Metaphors, and Broader Meanings of Global Impact**

I am quite open and frank about the fact that I firmly believe/feel that our nearly-50-year-old (founded in 1971; www.arnova.org; Smith, 1999a, 2013), organized, interdisciplinary field and emergent academic discipline of voluntaristics (or nonprofit sector, third sector, civil society studies; Smith, 2013, 2016a) currently needs a Kuhnian paradigm shift in thinking and theory regarding the role of MAS among all NPOS and in the larger VNPS as a societal sector worldwide (Kuhn, 1962). To advance that goal a bit, I not only have written the present paper, but also include the present section to suggest to readers that they might need to think more *outside the box* about these issues.

To aid interested readers in thinking more comprehensively and accurately about the nature, role, and potentials of MAS in the contemporary world and recent centuries, and also in voluntaristics, I suggest in this brief Section C several metaphors that attempt to convey such more expansive, realistic, and outside-the-box thinking, consistent with Kuhn's (1962) seminal book on scientific revolutions and the paradigm shifts that are centrally involved. In many such paradigm shifts, there is a root metaphor that conveys the essence of the shift in thinking needed. Sometimes the root metaphor is simple, but at other times quite complex.

In virtually all instances, scientific paradigm shifts involve paying increased or *any* attention observationally and theoretically to previously neglected phenomena, so as to have a broader, more comprehensive, and scientifically accurate view of some aspects of reality/nature, including human nature and human phenomena. In physics, studying relativistic phenomena was one contribution of Einstein's famous paradigm shifts (Pais, 1982), just as in biology, studying progressive, incremental evolution of living organisms of all kinds long term was Darwin's main contribution (Darwin & Wilson, 2005). In the socio-behavioral sciences, there have also been various key metaphors expressing paradigm shifts and greater scientific attention to previously neglected phenomena.

The concept of impact, as the word *impact* is used above and throughout here, requires some further discussion and elaboration beyond the relevant definitions in Section B above. Here are a few examples of metaphors that may help readers to understand my determination to foster a paradigm shift in voluntaristics regarding the theory and research on MAS and the entire VNPS.

1   *Astrophysical Dark Matter Metaphor*

In various articles and encyclopedia chapters, I have characterized MAS (e.g., Smith 1997c) as the *dark matter* of the voluntary nonprofit sector/VNPS (third sector, voluntary sector, charitable sector, civil society, civil society sector, tax-exempt sector, solidarity economy, social economy, etc.; see Smith, Stebbins, & Dover, 2006, p. 63), using an *astrophysical metaphor*. Astrophysicists have shown since about 1950 that the vast majority of physical matter in the universe is *dark* in the sense of being unseen or invisible, that is, not stars, planets, moons, etc. (Panek, 2011; Seymour, 2008). Thus, the most obvious and visible, bright matter/mass in the universe is only a tiny fraction (about 4%) of the reality of mass in the universe, because invisible dark matter is much more frequent, though still of unknown composition (Panek, 2011). For me, Volags/nonprofit agencies are the visible, bright matter of the VNPS or NPO universe, and the MAS, especially the small grassroots associations/GAs (Smith, 2000; 2004), are the dark, largely invisible dark matter, too often neglected by well-meaning but partially *MA-blind* voluntaristics scholars/academics (see Smith, 2000, pp. 33–64, Chapter 2).

2   Flat-Earth Maps Metaphor

Another metaphor that I have used seeks to convey the relative scholarly neglect of largely invisible MAS, especially small GAs, perceived by the author and some others is to refer to *flat-earth maps* of the VNPS (Smith, 2000, pp. 13–15). For nearly 200,000 years of humans as a species on earth, the (nearly?) universal perception by humans anywhere was that the earth was flat (not a globe), until *c*. 1500 CE (Zerubavel, 1992). Even after Magellan circumnavigated the globe in the early 1500s, the flat-earth perception was widespread among Europeans and actual flat-earth maps continued to be seen as accurate for a century or two more. Those flat-earth European maps omitted most of the world, just as omitting MAS in a map/view of the VNPS omits most of the VNPS world (see Smith, 2014c for estimates of the total of NPOS and MAS in the world recently).

In an attempt to reach the minds/brains of all voluntaristics scholars/academics, I have recently thought about various other relevant metaphors, and present a brief version of several of them here. All have in common illustrating overly simplistic thinking about some natural phenomena, thus neglecting a fuller, more comprehensive understanding of reality as befits science. Here, in no particular order, are a few of these new metaphors regarding the relative (*not* absolute) scholarly/academic neglect of MAS in both theory and research.

3   Global Animal/Plant Importance Metaphor

When laypeople think about the global importance of animals, they may often think first of the animals with larger mass, such as whales, elephants, hippopotamuses, rhinoceroses, and the like. In regard to plants, laypeople are also likely to think first of trees, as massive plants. But sophisticated scientific thinking/ theory, measurements, and extrapolation reveal a very different reality. Based on published data, Wikipedia (accessed January 28, 2018, for the term *biomass* [*ecology*]) states (p. 1) that, "Biomass is the mass of living biological organisms in a given area or ecosystem at a given time." Global biomass adds up all the biomass for a particular type of organism. In the table of Global biomass (p. 3), cattle comprise an estimated 520 million [metric] tonnes of biomass, but elephants and such are not mentioned. Tiny earthworms comprise a far larger estimated 3,800–7,600 metric tonnes of biomass. All minuscule global bacteria are further likely equal to or exceed total plant and animal global biomass. For me, viewing Volags/nonprofit agencies as the most important NPOs because of their larger size (in assets or income, buildings and equipment, paid staff, people allegedly served, fame or prestige, etc.) while neglecting usually smaller MAS, especially volunteer-based MAS with no paid staff (as true for most GAS), is an equivalent error of perception.

4   *Global Nonprofit Organizations Impact Metaphor*

When laypeople, and even most voluntaristics scholars/academics, think about all NPOs and the total VNPS in a society/nation or the whole world, Volags/nonprofit agencies usually seem to have the most impact because of the services they allegedly provide to many millions of recipients. Implicit in such simplistic thinking is the idea that such individual Volags or all of them together produce a huge total service benefit or impact for the population of a given society/nation and the whole of global society. However, that national or global service impact of Volags has not actually been demonstrated, when carefully assessed (see the next Section D). But just as elephants and trees do not dominate global biomass, while bacteria and earthworms do, so also do usually small and volunteer-run MAS (often GAS), especially 13 key types of MAS reviewed here, often local MAS as GAS/Grassroots associations (Smith, 1997a, 1997b, 1997c, 2000), have substantial and often enduring impacts on specific human societies/nations and often also on the whole of global human society. These social change and often ethical evolution impacts seem clearly more important than the cumulative, routine service impacts of Volags/NPAS, though doubtless many other scholars will dispute this.

5   *Metaphor of Global VNPS Origins of Nearly All Government Functions Services*

Most laypeople and even voluntaristics scholars/academics rarely if ever think about where all of the standard functions of governments have originated, taking for granted departments/agencies for health, transportation, defense/war, education, and the like. However, careful of examination of history, American history for example (e.g., de Tocqueville, 1976 [1845]), reveals that, with the exception of taxation (like the US Internal Revenue Service), nearly all major government functions/activities/services originated as innovations in the VNPS, often via an MA, not via a Volag or other NPO type. And in nearly every instance of a current government agency service or function, certain MAS in history had to make a substantial effort to get the specific government to accept taking on the new function/service, while defending the *status quo.*

For example, the federal Environmental Protection Agency in the USA grew clearly out of pressures and public consciousness-raising activities of the US environmental movement and its component MAS (Dunlap & Mertig, 1992, pp. 1–10). As another example, the US government's concern for the health and welfare of disabled persons grew out of an active disability rights movement begun decades earlier (Haskins & Stifle, 1979; Vaughn, 2003). At a broader level, US social policy and social welfare activities in general by the federal government grew out of various MAS and social movements comprised of these MAS (e.g., Lubove, 1968; Sanders, 1973; Skocpol, 1992).

6 Metaphor of Global Importance of Paid Work Activity and Work Organizations versus Global Importance of Leisure/Play Activity and Leisure MAS for a High Quality of Life and Felt Happiness

Volags/nonprofit agencies are clearly *work* organizations with paid staff mainly accomplishing their intended goals, sometimes with the help of affiliated Service Volunteer Programs (SVPs; Brudney et al., 2016). Hence, a paid staff worker in a Volag has a very different motivation and perception of his or her job than a volunteer doing the same activity in a VSP of the same Volag. Such major differences in work versus play/leisure orientations of participants result in conflicts and staff–volunteer potential interpersonal problems. Most people of working age in modern societies need a paying job, sometimes in NPOS, usually in Volags or larger MAS with some paid staff.

Comparisons of role/task/job satisfaction and more general life satisfaction/happiness between paid workers and volunteers nearly always find the volunteers more satisfied in a given Volag. So even if Volag services provided to non-staff/internal recipients (e.g., hospital patients) or external recipients (e.g., welfare service clients) *seem to be* more important than MA contributions/benefits/impacts to positive changes in national or global history, which the author here challenges, people need a balance of work and play/leisure if they are to lead happy lives with a satisfying Quality of Life (QOL). Research tends to show that volunteers in MAS and even volunteers in VSPS value and benefit from their roles in non-economic ways, and also in longer-term economic ways (Smith, 2016a, 2016b; Wilson et al., 2016).

7   *Metaphor that in Addition to Felt Satisfactions and Happiness being
     Higher on Average for People Affiliated with MAs as Volunteers
     than for People Affiliated with Volags as Paid Staff, MAs on Average
     Command More Commitment from Participants than Do Volags*

In many of the MA types reviewed here people have high commitment (possibly temporary), shown by (a) willingness to be volunteers (receiving no pay), (b) willingness to take risks with their lives and health, (c) willingness to risk losing some other paid job or and even family loss, (d) enjoyment of attempting to achieve non-financial/non-coercive goals that foster higher self-esteem, and (e) more opportunity for a sense of belonging and developing close and lasting friendships with other volunteers in a leisure setting (since all volunteer activity is done in leisure time; Robinson et al., 2016).

Recent reviews of happiness and life satisfaction/Quality of Life (QOL) research show the need for several factors that volunteering in MAs tend to provide routinely. For instance, quoting (with permission) from the relevant chapter in the *Palgrave handbook* (Smith, 2016b), "In his recent book *Flourish*, Seligman (2012) elaborates on this vital engagement aspect of finding/making the good life, based on his review and study of positive psychology. He argues for the mantra *PERMA*, spelled out as Positive emotions, Engagement, Relationships, Meaning, and Accomplishment as the necessary elements of 'a life of profound fulfillment.' Many people find such fulfillment through volunteering and/or citizen participation, including religious congregation/association activity, among other meaningful activities."

D   **Historical Background of MA Impact Research**

Serious research attention to the impact of MAs is a very recent phenomenon, although evaluation research on the impact of organizations in general goes back a bit further in time, roughly to the 1950s (e.g., Comrey, Pfiffner, & High, 1952; Georgopoulos & Tannenbaum, 1957). However, this impact/effectiveness subfield of organizational research mainly proliferated from the late 1960s and into the 1970s (Cameron, 1982). In the USA, for instance, in the first edition of the literature review book on organizations in general by Hall (1972, pp. 96–102), seven pages of text refer to the effectiveness of organizations. He uses Etzioni's (1964, p. 8) definition of effectiveness, as "the degree to which [an organization] realizes its goals." However, this is not a simple matter, because there are usually "multiple and often conflicting goals," some of which may be covert or even not understood by the organization's current (or original) leaders.

Various other organization scholars wrote whole monographs on organizational effectiveness at about the same time (e.g., Goodman, Pennings, & Associates, 1977; Price, 1968; Spray, 1976), but *all ignored NPOs, especially MAs*. Kanter and Brinkerhoff (1981) wrote the first chapter in the *Annual Review of Sociology* on organizational effectiveness, early in the 1980s. The first comprehensive bibliography of organizational effectiveness research (Cameron, 1982) identified over 500 relevant documents, including a few early studies of effectiveness in associations (see below).

Identifying the various goals of an organization and their relative priorities, let alone for a more informal group like a GA, is itself problematic. Hall (1972, pp. 79–96) devotes nearly twenty pages to such issues, distinguishing operative (*de facto*) from official (*de jure*) goals, citing other key scholars (e.g., Perrow, 1961; Simon, 1964; Thompson & McEwen, 1958). Included in these pages (pp. 87–94) is a discussion of goal changes in an organization, which Hall views as resulting from both direct and indirect environmental factors, as well as from internal factors (see Smith, with Stebbins et al., 2016, Section D, #1). As Thompson and McEwen (1958) have discussed, goal-setting in any organization is an interactive process that usually takes account both of internal factors, including leader motivations, perceptions, and prior experiences, and also the environment.

The earliest careful research evaluation of MA effectiveness likely was by Sills (1957), who studied a national health association (The March of Dimes) in the USA. Other early publications on assessing the effectiveness of NPOs, especially MAs, include Horowitz and Sorensen (1978), Simpson and Gulley (1962), Tannenbaum (1961), and Warner (1967).

Clotfelter (1992) edited a book on "who benefits from the nonprofit sector," looking for systematic, positive impacts on the poor and disadvantaged in America. However, there is little or no discussion of MAs, only Volags. He and his contributors found very little impact. In his Chapter 1 (p. 22), he wrote by way of conclusions that, "there is also evidence that relatively few nonprofit institutions serve the poor as a primary clientele." Clotfelter also makes the important observation (p. 23) that, "we have only the most rudimentary understanding of the outputs of nonprofit institutions—their forms, how broadly they are distributed, and how they should be valued."

More recently, Diaz (2002) wrote a chapter on "the contributions of the nonprofit sector" in America. Like Clotfelter, he also focuses mainly on Volags, seen as generally making only a relatively small effort recently for the goal of helping the poor and the disadvantaged (p. 519). However, Diaz has a section (pp. 524–529) on what he calls *indigenous agencies*, which refers to MAS as well as some Volags comprised of people from poor and disadvantaged backgrounds. He states (p. 524), "[t]his suggests that the only portion of the non-profit sector that pays consistent attention to the neediest communities is the portion created and led by members of those communities themselves" (that is, MAS). He discusses briefly (pp. 525–528) both African-American and Mexican-American MAS as mutual aid or member service providers.

Diaz (2002) also summarizes some major types of contributions made by indigenous agencies (MAS) (pp. 528–529): services to the needy, public education, advocacy with the government, leadership development, and greater involvement of disadvantaged people in the American political process. Given these conclusions, it should be little wonder that, in Section E of this paper, we are at pains to indicate how much social movements comprised of disadvantaged people have achieved in the past century or two as key impacts of MAS.

Smith (1973b) presented several chapters focused on the impact of voluntary action (equivalent to all of the VNPS), including MAS. The chapter with the broadest scope was entitled "The impact of the voluntary sector on society" (reprinted as Smith, 2001). Ten different, broad types of impact were identified by qualitative content analysis of the extant research literature:

1. Providing "society with a large variety of partially tested social innovations, from which business, government, and other institutions can select and institutionalize those innovations which seem most promising" (p. 388).
2. Providing "countervailing definitions of reality and morality—ideologies, perspectives, and worldviews that frequently challenge the prevailing assumptions about what exists and what is good and what should be done in society" (p. 388).
3. Providing "the play element in society, especially as the search for novelty, beauty, recreation, and fun for their own sake may be collectively organized" (p. 389).
4. Providing satisfaction of "some of the human needs for affiliation, approval, and so on" (p. 389).
5. Preservation of older "values, ways of life, ideas, beliefs, artifacts, and other productions of the mind, heart, and hand of man from earlier times so that this great variety of human culture is not lost to future generations" (p. 391).
6. Providing "an embodiment and representation in society of the sense of mystery, wonder, and the sacred" (p. 392).

7. Liberating "the individual and [permitting] him or her the fullest possible measure of expression of personal capacities and [growth] potentialities within an otherwise constraining social environment" (p. 392).
8. Providing "a source of 'negative feedback' for society as a whole, especially with regard to the directions taken by the major institutions of society such as government and business" (p. 394).
9. Providing "support ... specifically to the economic system of a society, especially a modern industrial [or post-industrial, information-service] society" (p. 396).
10. Providing "an important *latent* resource for all kinds of goal attainment in the interests of society as a whole" (p. 396).

For all of the above positive impacts there can also be corresponding "negative consequences in certain circumstances and with regard to certain values" (Smith, 1973b, p. 397). Eng et al. (2016) explore this dark side of associations. Smith (2018a, 2018b) provides an overview of how fundamentally deviant voluntary associations (DVAs), such as revolutionary and social movement MAs, have had major impacts on human history and on progressive sociocultural change and ethical evolution in many societies for the past 200 years especially. The *deviance paradox* of DVAs, identified by Smith (2018b), is that nearly all DVAs have been initially resisted and stigmatized both by relevant governments and by the general public, even though many dissenting DVAs have turned out to be very positive forces for sociocultural change in the longer term and in the judgment of history (e.g., the anti-slavery movement, the women's rights movement, the trade/labor union movement, etc.).

The final report of the Filer Commission in the USA (Commission on Private Philanthropy and Public Needs, 1975; abbreviated as CPPPN), with which the author was affiliated, presented its own version of the *underlying functions, social roles*, or *societal benefits* of voluntary groups, and hence of the VNPS (pp. 41–46):

- Initiating new ideas and processes.
- Developing public policy.
- Supporting minority or local interests.
- Providing services that the government is constitutionally barred from providing (e.g., aspects of religion).
- Overseeing government.
- Overseeing the marketplace.
- Bringing the sectors together.

- Giving aid abroad.
- Furthering active citizenship and altruism.

Douglas (1983) discusses the many reasons why the VNPS, and especially the charitable or philanthropic part of the VNPS, is valuable in societies. A special role of the VNPS that he identifies, among others, is the provision of social group (MA) support for people having different values and opinions/social orientations in a large, diverse, and complex modern society (ibid., p. 47). Thus, the VNPS supports both diversity and intellectual/ideological freedom in non-authoritarian societies.

O'Neill (1989) has a special section (pp. 13–17) of his Chapter 1 entitled, "Societal importance of the third sector," which goes beyond the mere citing of numbers and dollars involved earlier in this chapter. He notes (pp. 13–14) de Tocqueville's (1976 [1845]) various positive statements about American MAS and their benefits for society. O'Neill then reviews other benefits of the VNPS or NPOS for society, including Smith's list of roles or functions (in 1973b, reprinted in Smith, 2001), listed just above. O'Neill (1989, p. 15) notes that economic theories of the VNPS "have stressed that nonprofits provide a level of collective and individual goods beyond that which government and business will provide, goods that do not have enough money-making potential to attract business and that have insufficient popular appeal to attract the mass of voters." O'Neill (ibid., p. 17) also notes that, "Voluntary associations play an important role in leadership development for those with little access to such roles in business and government organizations," a point omitted in Smith's list. O'Neill (ibid.) closes this section by noting, "Nonprofits daily assist millions of people in need through health care, social service, and legal assistance agencies."

E   Key Association Types for Global Impact

There are various ways that this very long section of the paper could have been organized, but the author chose to focus on some key institutional areas of human societies in order to review impacts. Anthropologists and sociologists have long used these institutional areas to order comprehensively the broad activity/normative patterns, social structures, or cultural *lifeways* of all human societies (e.g., Fardon et al., 2012; Kroeber, 1948; Lowie, 1948; Parsons, 1966; Scott, 1995; Turner, 2003). Other book authors or editors have made a similar choice, with less variety, when attempting broad overviews of the VNPS and its impact (e.g., Clotfelter, 1992; O'Neill, 2002; Powell & Steinberg, 2006; Salamon, 2012).

The methodology for studying MA outcomes and impacts in this paper is basically qualitative (e.g., Herman & Renz, 2008), though some quantitative research is also cited. I take this approach because my central concern is with the long-term, thus historical, impact or influence of MAS as an NPO type, not the specific, short-term impact or influence of particular MAS. Given the mainly qualitative nature of the research reviewed in this chapter, the take-away content for the reader will likely be qualitative as well. More quantitative evaluations of associations, volunteer service programs (VSPS), and paid-staff nonprofit agencies, have been done over the past four or more decades (Forbes, 1998; Khandker, Koolwal, & Samad, 2010; Rossi, Lipsey, & Freeman, 2003; Wholey, Hatry, & Newcomer, 2010).

However, some experts have raised serious questions about the validity of such findings (e.g., Flynn & Hodgkinson, 2002), while applied researcher-practitioners find great value in such evaluations and their results. In addition, economists and others have demonstrated the monetary value of volunteering, imputing (assigning) an hourly wage-estimate to various volunteer work activities, as an alternative approach to assessing the impact of volunteering (see More-Hollerweger et al., 2016). However, this is a form of *input evaluation*, and does not address the more important questions of whether the hours of volunteer time provide any useful *outputs*, let alone valuable *outcomes* or causal impacts.

The 13 key types of MAS for global impact are roughly ordered below in terms of descending or decreasing degree of disruptive impact on society and intentional violence (as contrasted with government or general public violence used against them) during their main period of activity.

1 Revolutionary, Guerrilla, and Civil War MAS

Most scholars who study social movements/SMS and/or social movement organizations/SMOS tend to do so considering such MAS in democratic political regimes (Tilly, 2004). When SMS/SMOS are studied in authoritarian or totalitarian regimes, past or present, there is a tendency to ignore the SMS/SMOS that often precipitate or at least organize the revolutions that occur from time to time in these states. There is also a tendency by voluntaristics scholars to ignore such revolutionary and guerrilla MAS and their roles in guerrilla wars or civil wars.

Tilly (1993, p. 10) argues that revolutions can occur for a variety of underlying reasons, some of which he (1993, p. 16) refers to as *revolutionary situations*, such as top-down seizures of power, coups, civil wars, limited revolts, and widespread popular revolutions. He defines (p. 16) a two-dimensional graph of types of revolutions in terms of (1) the degree of split in the polity, and (2) the degrees of transfer of power in the polity. Skocpol (1979) provides a structural analysis of the origins of the social revolutions in France, Russia, and China. Goldstone (1991) also provides a structural analysis of the English, French, and two Asian revolutions, but adds a final section on ideology and cultural struggles. He notes (p. 421) that various ideologically based groups (MAS) may form once the state control breaks down.

Colburn (1994) focuses on twenty-two more recent revolutions in poor countries after World War II (1945–1983), usually involving a break with dominant colonial powers. He argues (pp. 42–43) that these more recent revolutions were unusual in the key role of socialist ideology (*the vogue of socialism*; p. 99) espoused by the leaders involved and also by liberation/revolutionary SMS/SMOS, when present. Colburn wrote (pp. 43–44), "Insurgents were indispensable, not just to tackle the might of colonial armies but to enlist widespread public support for their cause as well. The struggle for liberation was always as much a political as a military challenge. [...] Political organization and leadership were necessary." Although Colburn did not use the terminology, the organizations involved were clearly revolutionary or liberation SMOS, and hence MAS, using present terms (see also p. 47).

Some of the recent anti-colonial revolutions in Latin America, the Middle East, Africa, and Asia have involved armed struggles, and sometimes guerrilla wars, fostered by SMS/MOS with Marxist/Socialist ideologies (see many examples of books cited in the bibliography of Colburn, 1994). For instance, Gilbert (1991) describes and discusses the Sandinista National Liberation Front (FSLN) guerrilla SMO that successfully precipitated the revolution in Nicaragua. Martin (1981) does the same thing for the Chimurenga [guerrilla] War of revolution in Zimbabwe (previously Rhodesia). The much earlier American Revolution had a similar origin in SM/SMO MAS, like the Committees of Correspondence and the local colonial militia (Gross, [1976] 2002; Maier, 1992). Castro (1999) gives a general overview of guerrilla SMS/SMOS in Latin America. Landau (1993) presents a similar review for Central American revolutions. Ness (2009) has edited a 4300-page *International encyclopedia of revolution and protest*, with very many examples of SMS/SMO MAS.

Rather different have been the activities of social bandits and low-level peasant resistance MAS in the past two centuries. Unlike the riots and rebellions of the prior section, these actions have often had a GA at their core, but did not really seek to change their existing societal government (Crummey, 1986; Hobsbawm, 1965). Some of their activities involved theft to support an underground or outlaw lifestyle.

Making analytical and also practical distinctions among MAS involved in revolutions, guerrilla resistance, guerilla war campaigns, insurgency, citizen

HISTORICAL IMPACTS OF VOLUNTARY ASSOCIATIONS 27

militias, and/or terrorism is difficult (Polk, 2008; Rich & Duyvesteyn, 2014; Schmid, 2013; Shultz & Dew, 2006). Often these terms are used loosely and virtually synonymously. The MAs involved may have multiple roles at a given time and/or shift from one of these roles as their main activity to another main role or to a different set of roles or pattern of activities at later times. *What is clear for present purposes is that the core groups involved are MAs, though usually fundamentally deviant MAs* (Eng et al., 2016; Smith, 2000, 2018a forthcoming; Smith with Van Puyvelde, 2016). Also quite clear *is that the participants in MAs are usually unpaid volunteers*, though some may receive subsistence gifts in kind (e.g., food, drink, temporary lodging).

All of the categories of deviant MAs (or deviant voluntary associations/ DVAs; Smith, 2018a) discussed in this sub-section above have tended to have significant impacts, and sometimes huge impacts, in their nations of activity, based on qualitative historical accounts. The encyclopedia edited by Ness (2009) provides ample multinational case study evidence of such impact, as does the handbook by Rich and Duyvesteyn (2014). Polk (2008) provides a historical overview of insurgency and guerrilla wars in the past few centuries. When compared to similar qualitative evaluations of the impacts of most types of Volags anytime anywhere, these DVAs seem far more important historically.

2 *Underground Political Resistance MAs in Foreign-Army-Occupied Nations/Societies*

In the Introduction to the massive, Smith, Stebbins, and Grotz-edited (2016, p. 1), *Palgrave handbook of volunteering, citizen participation, and nonprofit associations*, the following general perspective on MAs was presented in a manner relevant to this subsection, as follows (quoted here with permission):

> Formal volunteering takes place in an overwhelming variety of membership associations (MAs) worldwide, as well as in volunteer service programs (VSPs). MAs focus on every topical area, idea, belief, issue, and problem in contemporary nations having non-totalitarian political regimes. In writing/compiling this Handbook, the editors are acting on their belief that MAs are the central, vital, driving force of the global Voluntary Nonprofit Sector (VNPS)—its 'soul' and the roots of its values, passions, and ethics (Eberly & Streeter, 2002; Rothschild & Milofsky, 2006). While the review chapters written for this volume are intended to be objective, scientific treatises, we Editors are motivated significantly by our values and passions for MAs and their volunteers, acting in their leisure time, and what they do for the world. Not all of MA impacts are beneficial for people and societies in general (see Smith, Stebbins, & Grotz,

2016, Chapters 52 and 53), but *most* impacts are beneficial in the longer term in our view (see op. cit., Chapter 52; and Smith 2017d [the present article]).

Also, in section C of this paper, I noted several aspects of the broader impact of voluntary action/the VNPS on society that are also relevant in this subsection. In Smith (1973), three general types of impacts of voluntary action and MAS help explain why underground resistance groups/MAS arose in all Nazi-occupied European nations in World War II (World War II; e.g., Batinic, 2015; Eisner, 2005; Gildea, 2015; Hoogstraten, 2008; Lampe & Riis-Jorgensen, 2014; Mastny, 1971; Novacek, 2012; Pavone & Levy, 2014):

(a) Providing "*countervailing definitions of reality and morality*": The occupying Nazi regime, after conquest of a country or a region of it (e.g., Vichy France), had their own, dominating, rapacious, destructive, inhumane version of morality that promoted Hitler and his version of the Third Reich in exquisite detail above all, denying any value to the lives or health/social welfare of native citizens or any other non-German residents of the nation. By contrast, underground (UG) resistance participants/activists, *always volunteers*, joined UG Resistance (UGR) MAS that had highly *deviant* definitions of reality and morality, suggesting that the Nazi war machine and occupiers should be stopped or hindered by any means possible, including murder, sabotage, theft, lies, fake ID papers, and so on. Based on this deviant (from the standpoint of the occupying Nazis) view of reality and morality, volunteer participants in UGR MAS (essentially, *de facto* members) risked their own lives and health; that of their family/relatives, neighbors, and friends; their jobs, normal lives, leisure activities, and homes; their access to food, drink, clothing, and medicine; and their freedom. *In essence, they risked everything of value in their lives in order to resist what they deeply felt was the ultimate evil of the Nazi regime.*

Unfortunately, with their usual efficiency and effectiveness, as shown in the broader holocaust extinction program, the Nazi SS and Gestapo captured, tortured, and killed probably 90%+ of all active UGR MA partisans, and this high success rate for the Nazis was widely known to the partisans. Such underground resistance MAS and GAS were likely the most dangerous MAS/GAS of which one could ever be a member (Aubrac, 1993; Kedward, 1991; Mastny, 1971). It is hard (impossible?) to imagine a Volag that could command this level of personal commitment and sacrifice from its paid staff, or the members of its VSP, if any.

(b) Providing "*a source of 'negative feedback' for society as a whole*," in this case, total rejection and attempted destruction of the perceived horrors of the occupying Nazi regime as the dominating "society." Crucially, this highly deviant (from the Nazi perspective), negative feedback came not in the form of thoughts or mere words, spoken or written (although underground newspapers/newssheets were printed in some nations; Lampe & Riis-Jorgensen, 2014). Rather, the resoundingly active rejection usually came via often-violent counteractions of the Nazi occupying regime, its staff, its organizational structures, its offices and barracks, and any useful facilities or equipment commandeered (stolen) by the Nazis. Resistance partisans in several nations helped Jews to safety, keeping them from Nazi extermination camps, at least for a while. In addition, many UGR MA partisans helped downed/crashed pilots from the Allies, and protected them, returning them usually to England for future active war-making against the broader Nazi war effort (Eisner, 2005).

(c) Providing "*an important latent resource for all kinds of goal attainment in the interests of society as a whole*." In a nutshell, whatever kind of special collective problem arises, some kind of MA can deal with it, or at least attempt to do so. MAS are infinitely flexible in terms of the goal or goals they can seek. There are literally no limits on their goals. An MA only requires a few (actually, only two; Smith, 1967) like-minded people to form and begin to act: no money, no other resources, no permission, no government recognition or registration, no external recognition or permission at all is required, even though it may be prescribed by law in a given nation or region (e.g., in China now; Smith with Zhao, 2016).

Such UGR MAS can be seen alternatively as another kind of SMS/SMOS, in this case, as guerrilla or terrorist MAS, both as deviant national or regional MAS, and also their local cells (deviant GAS) in Nazi-occupied European nations during WWII (e.g., Kedward, 1991). Although these were revolutionary MAS in principle, they mainly confined their activities to local sabotage against Nazi barracks and installations as well as against Nazi-controlled logistics/equipment, and performing information gathering on Nazi troop movements for the Allies (Aubrac, 1993; Kedward, 1991; Lampe & Riis-Jorgensen, 2014; Rings, 1982). Gildea (2015, Chap. 13) discussed in detail how the French Resistance aided the Allies on the ground from D-Day onward. (See also Funk, 1992, on how the French Resistance aided the Allied invasion in 1944.) One observer said that the World War II Resistance in general was worth in total several military divisions over the duration of the war. There is a substantial book literature (nearly

2000 documents) in a bibliography on Nazism, resistance, and holocaust in WWII (Laska, 1985).

3　　*Terrorist MAs*

Terrorist MAs seek to have political influence/impact and change the political system by use of public violence, aiming to generate widespread fear or even panic among the public of a target nation/society (e.g., Chalk, 2012; Combs & Slann, 2007; Schmid, 2013). Such MAs are of the same radical and violent nature as Underground Political Resistance (UPR) MAs just discussed, and tend to have similar lack of long-term success on average. Indeed, the occupying Nazi Germans saw UPR MAs and their active members as simply terrorists (Gildea, 2015). Nonetheless, terrorist MA violence gains great notoriety in the mass media and arouses substantial fear in the population (e.g., Al Qaeda: Gunaratna, 2002; Wright, 2006), which is indeed a kind of widespread emotional impact in various affected countries.

Jackson et al. (2016, dust cover text) argued that, "Terrorism and the war on terror has affected virtually every aspect of modern life." That conclusion seems excessive, especially regarding terrorism itself. Note that in this quotation the *war on terror* is distinguished from actual terrorism itself. Although some writers/observers spoke of a *war on terror* or *war against the terrorists* beginning in the 1980s (e.g., Klein, 2005; Rivers, 1986), the war on terror is commonly dated from right after the Al Qaeda attack on the twin towers of New York City on September 11, 2001 (Jacobson & Colon, 2008; Wright, 2017). The war on terror has harmed and diminished American ideals, according to Mayer (2008) and others.

Most importantly, since terrorism itself (*not* including the *war on terror* or war against terrorism as essentially government responses to terrorism) is violence aimed at political change, the actual results of the intended political impact of terrorist MAs on average are not substantial on average (Chalk, 2012; Combs & Slann, 2007; Jackson, 2016). It is crucial to separate recent Al Qaeda terrorism from all other, prior and subsequent, terrorism. For instance, the terrorist MAs in Northern Ireland (IRA, PIRA) over many decades in the 20th century accomplished few of their intended goals (Coogan, 2002; English, 2004; McKearney, 2011). This low average impact of terrorism *per se* occurs especially because the governments and military in affected/target nations strongly resist and seek out/punish suspected terrorists and terrorist MAs (Jackson, 2016).

Very different from the *orthodox terrorism* of MAs as sketched above, *state terrorism* also exists, in which national governments and their paid covert agents, not genuine MAs (but which may be utilized as fake cover NPOs), use terrorism to attempt to harm and often control or dominate other societies/

nations (Blakeley, 2007; Feldmann, 2016, Part III, pp. 157–212). Since about 1970, state terrorism has often been used by some larger nations of the Global North against nations of the Global South (Blakeley, 2007; Jackson, 2016). State terrorism is more likely to use torture and other extreme methods against opponents, although orthodox terrorism has few limits in its use of violence, especially mass public violence (Blakeley, 2007). The true identity/origins of state terrorist groups can sometimes be kept secret from enemy/target nations, and state terrorism has the great advantage for the sponsoring nation of being much cheaper and less risky than conventional wars against an enemy nation.

4   *Hate Groups as MAs*

Because the aims/goals of Hate MAs are often vague and general (such as, "eliminate all the" Jews or black/colored people or foreigners), assessing their impact is particularly difficult. But there is little doubt that some hate groups in some societies/nations have fostered hatred in the general population to some extent and have harmed some targets of hate, sometimes engaging in public violence. Authors of major books on hate MAs such as the Ku Klux Klan (KKK) or American militias (Dees, 1997; Southers, 2013; Stern, 1996) tend to over-emphasize the dangers posed by such MAs, encouraging counter-terrorism efforts, and perhaps to sell more books.

Hate groups as MAs often overlap with terrorist MAs (as discussed above), sometimes involve political parties (covered below), such as Hitler's Nazi party (McDonough, 2003) or other extreme right-wing parties (Waltman, 2014), and are sometimes deviant religious MAs (Stern, 2003), such as recent Al Qaeda, Islamic terrorist MAs (Avalos, 2005, pp. 239–299; Napoleoni, 2005, pp. 99–108; Wright, 2006). Hate MAs are clearly also deviant voluntary associations in general, as #5 below, active mainly as a phenomenon since 1800. The KKK in the USA, from the later 1800s down to the present, is one well-known US example of a Hate MA (Sims, 1996; Tucker, 1991). A related subtype of Hate MAs is Skinhead youth gangs in the USA (Hamm, 1994; Christensen, 1994). Since about 1960 in the USA, paramilitary militia MAs have been serious white racist hate groups (Abanes, 1996; Dees, 1997; Levitas, 2002; Stern, 1996). Abanes (1996) traced the ideological roots of American paramilitia MAs to white supremacist theories and the anti-Semitism of centuries ago.

However, an objective if qualitative assessment of Hate MAs must be that they and their actions rarely accomplish their broader stated aims of eliminating (killing or deporting) or imprisoning many or all of their targets of hate as a category. Hate MAs mainly talk hatred and spend much time training for and discussing an expected future race war or the overthrow of the federal government. Episodes of actual physical harm to targets of hatred tend to be few in numbers, and mass violence is very rare, although it does occur occasionally with great mass media notoriety. Even strong hate groups usually do not endure long in their influence, as they arouse significant opposition from the government and often the public if/when they commit violence and are identified as the perpetrators (Tucker, 1991). However, active and enduring hatred of some category of different others (by race, religion, national origin, gender preference, etc.) seems to be a recurring human characteristic, especially among the poor, less educated, and socially alienated.

5   Deviant Voluntary Associations in General as MAs

Deviant voluntary associations (DVAs) is a category that refers not to MA purposes/goals, but rather to whether these purposes/goals are currently acceptable (as opposed to deviant or rule-breaking) in the current society/nation-state in which the MA is embedded. This broad type of MAs overlaps conceptually with all four MA sub-types reviewed above. Some MA sub-types reviewed in this article are inherently deviant in this sense: revolutionary, guerrilla, and civil war MAs; underground political resistance groups; Terrorist MAs; Hate groups as MAs. These four subtypes of MAs were reviewed separately in some detail above because of their significant and often substantial global impacts. The next subtype, social movements/social movement organizations (SMOs) as MAs, are usually perceived initially also as deviant or rule-breaking, but not always. The other sub-types of MAs reviewed here below can be deviant/rule-breaking or not, but are usually more acceptable in their societies, with dark side exceptions noted.

Rather than write at greater length here about DVAs in general, sections of other documents by the author and others that review this topic and relevant research literature are briefly quoted below. There are very few books that attempt to present and assess the nature and impact of DVAs, although there are a few edited compendia that include a variety of DVAs (e.g., George & Wilcox, 1996; Kephart & Zellner, 1994). The most recent general review chapter on the topic is by Eng et al. (2016). The historical background section of this review chapter states the following (quoted here with permission):

> Although no solid empirical evidence exists to our knowledge, it is likely that there has been some deviance and misconduct in certain MAs at certain times since associations first came into widespread existence about 10,000 years ago (Smith 1997b; see also [Harris et al., 2016, pp. 23–58]). Wherever there are humans and human groups, some deviance and

HISTORICAL IMPACTS OF VOLUNTARY ASSOCIATIONS

misconduct occur at times (Smith, 2008a, 2008b). In the major ancient civilizations of the West, there are a few studies by historians of clearly deviant voluntary associations.

JOSEPHUS, 1960, P. 528; KLOPPENBORG & WILSON, 1996, CHAP. 7

The voluntary nonprofit sector has long been seen as angelic in the United States (Smith, 2000, 2008a), but this was not always the case. For nearly the first 100 years of America as a nation there were negative views of independent associations. Stern (2013, pp. 54–57) discusses the historical development of a positive image for the MAs and other nonprofit organizations in America, where the initial perceptions were quite negative from the mid-1700s to the mid-1800s. In the United States more recently, associations and nonprofit agencies have long been seen as embodying the moral high ground.

HOLLOWAY, 1998; SEE ALSO SMITH, STEBBINS, & GROTZ, 2016, CHAP. 49

The larger VNPS is a more recent concept, mainly developed in the 1970s and thereafter (Hall, 1992; Smith, Reddy, & Baldwin, 1972; Smith, 2016a; Smith with Dixon, 1973; see also Harris et al., 2016, pp. 23–58). Along with this new concept came such altruistic perceptions of the sector as promoting generosity, forgiveness, virtue, philanthropy, intergroup cooperation and the like (American Sociological Association, 2013). But Smith (2008b) has argued that the *dark side of goodness* of the nonprofit sector, encompassing organizational crime and misconduct, has not been adequately addressed and explored (cf., Smith [2018a, 2018d]). In the past decade or so, several major books have appeared with a focus on the dark side of the VNPS, often with a title stressing the word *charity* and discussing the United States (Fishman, 2007; Snyder, 2011; Stern, 2013; Wagner, 2000; White, 2006; Zack, 2003). In a sense, such books follow up on a much earlier chapter in Bakal (1979) on misconduct by charities. On a more global basis, several recent books also deal with misconduct and corruption in transnational relief and development assistance NPOs, including various major MAs (de Waal, 1997; Hancock, 1992; Holmén, 2010; Kennedy, 2004), as discussed in Smith, with Eng, and Albertson (2016).

Smith, with Eng and Albertson (2016), is another recent publication by the author on DVAs. One forthcoming book by Smith on DVAs (2018a) delves into nearly ninety empirically grounded hypotheses supported by selected qualitative studies in the past 800 years in various countries, but mainly the USA. A related forthcoming book (Smith, 2018b—*Nonprofits daring to be different: Changing the world through collective deviant voluntary action*) reviews selected DVAs from several countries, with the DVAs categorized as either *noxious, eccentric,* or *dissenting,* with the third category referring to SMOS.

The prospectus for that book (Smith, 2018b) states the following (quoted here with permission):

> This is the first scholarly book that provides an analytical overview of deviance/rule-breaking/norm-violations in and by many different types of voluntary associations through historical time and across different societies/nations that are *un*conventional and *fundamentally deviant,* usually covert and stigmatized. The book's main purpose is to bring a kind of theoretical order out of a rarely-studied *category* of human groups that seemingly manifests only chaos and madness in human societies and history. To most observers, the huge diversity and variety of these Deviant Voluntary Associations (DVAs) across historical times and societies beggars the mind to make any sense of them. These DVAs are clearly nonprofit/voluntary associations (Smith 2015b), with memberships and involving mainly or only volunteers. But DVAs are **not** nonprofit agencies with paid staff, seeking mainly to serve and benefit selected external (non-member) recipients or the larger society.
>
> SMITH 2015C

Quoting further from the prospectus for Smith (2018b),

> The book's main argument is that such rule-breaking (deviance) by DVAs in any society or historical time period follows some discernable patterns that can be induced as generalizations and take-away lessons for the reader by careful study of the relevant phenomena. Looking forward in time, such generalizations can be seen as the tentative hypotheses of a grounded theory (Glaser & Strauss, 1967), derived creatively from qualitative ethnographies, biographies/autobiographies, and histories in the published research literature. Further, such generalizations have significant value for association leaders, law enforcement professionals, and policy-makers in general in any society.

Continuing, "Each main chapter begins with a brief description of some well-studied Deviant Voluntary Association (DVA), such as the German Nazi Party (1921–1933) as a revolutionary political party, the Pennsylvania Abolition Society from the late 1700s to the mid-1800s as a social movement organization seeking to abolish slavery in the state of Pennsylvania and eventually throughout the USA, and the Oneida Community in New York (1848–1881) as

HISTORICAL IMPACTS OF VOLUNTARY ASSOCIATIONS 35

a residential commune practicing a deviant lifestyle that included a kind of sexual freedom for all residents. Generalizations are made as hypotheses in each chapter and especially in summary chapters of each Part of the book. The final two chapters discuss efforts directed towards government regulation and self-regulation of the nonprofit sector, including DVAs and their actual or potential misconduct. The importance of civil liberties and freedoms for the continued vitality of associations and democracy is emphasized."

6 Social Movements and Social Movement Organizations (SMOs) as MAS

In the author's view, the single greatest type of average global historical impact of MAs has been in the realm of sociocultural change for greater human rights, humane values, democracy, and ethical evolution, meaning increasing attention to ethics and altruism in sociocultural systems/societies/nations (Broom, 2004; Kitcher, 2011). All of the latter, interrelated value concepts and goals have been promoted and often achieved though the activities of MAs, especially in the past 200 or so years. In particular, social movement organizations (SMOs; Lofland, 1996) as MAs have been in the forefront of conceptualizing, defining, advocating for, and, through political pressure for government legislation, establishing a variety of human rights since about 1800 CE in industrial/modern and post-industrial/post-modern nations (Tilly, 2004, 2007).

In his review of social movements (SMS) and SMOS in the period 1768–2004, Tilly (2004, Chap. 2) argues cogently that SMs first arose in the late 18th century and early 19th century, especially in Britain, France, and the USA. Since the agrarian economic revolution beginning about 5000 years ago (Nolan & Lenski, 2006), wealthy elites, usually hereditary royalty and other nobility, have controlled large tracts of land, especially in states and later in nation-states (Johnson & Earle, 1987, pp. 303, 318–319, 324; Service, 1975). These tracts of land were worked/farmed by poor, undernourished, hereditary peasants, who were taxed heavily and dominated by their landlords.

Peasant protests, riots, and even rebellions have occurred occasionally as a result of such treatment over the past five millennia in agrarian/peasant regimes, but they have been very rare (Scott, 1985, p. 29; Service, 1975, pp. 301–303). And "when they do appear the revolts that develop are nearly always crushed unceremoniously," with few or no lasting gains for the peasants (Scott, 1985, p. 29). Such rebellions, riots, and uprisings have nearly always been rather spontaneous events of emotion-based collective behavior, *not* guided by SMOS or other MAS. This latter is a key point: MAs *have made the difference historically between centuries, even millennia, of* unsuccessful *resistance/protests/rebellions against oppressive and autocratic authorities, versus more historically recent* successful *resistance as emotion-based collective action and especially,* successful *instrumental sociocultural change attempts, especially through SMS/SMOS.*

Only with the rise of early democratic nations in Western Europe and the USA in the period 1775–1825 could SMS and their constituent SMOS arise and persist, according to Tilly (2004, Chap. 1). Tilly (2004, p. 12) states: "Democratization promotes the formation of social movements." Effective civil liberties are a crucial component of democracy, if SMOS are to have significant impact (Bresler, 2004, Bresler et al., 2016; Inazu, 2012; McWhirter, 1994; Scherr, 1989). Looked at from the opposite perspective, "[t]he relaxation of repression [by the government] promoted social movement activity" in Britain in the early 19th century (Tilly, 2004, p. 31). In his Chapter 6, Tilly (2004) expands on his argument that *significant democracy is necessary for SMS/SMOS to arise and persist.* He notes (p. 125) that, "as of 2004 most of the world's people still lacked access to social movements as a way to voice popular claims." Yet SMS/SMOS "do not necessarily espouse or promote democracy" (Tilly, 2004, p. 126). "From early on, relatively democratic movements regularly provoked undemocratic countermovements...." (ibid.).

Contrary to Tilly's thesis above, there is clear evidence that *SMS/SMOS can arise and be successful at times in totalitarian and even in less restrictive authoritarian regimes* (O'Brien & Li, 2006; Smith with Zhao, 2016; Tilly, 1993. This is especially true if one considers the SMS/SMOS involved in revolutions (Colburn, 1994; Tilly, 1993) and guerrilla wars/campaigns (Corbett, 1986; Landau, 1993).

As Mati et al. (2016) show, *SMOS are almost invariably MAS, not paid-staff Volags aimed at helping non-members by providing services.* SMOS are distinguished from other MAS by seeking significant sociocultural or socio-political change in their own societies, and also by using unconventional (non-electoral and non-lobbying) tactics to achieve their goals—direct action, strikes, protest rallies or marches, intimidation, and even violence (e.g., Jenkins & Klandermans, 1995, p. 277; Meyer, 2007; Smith, Stebbins, and Dover, 2006, pp. 213–214). Piven and Cloward (1979) made a notable case long ago, buttressed again more recently by Piven (2006), that violence and disruption by SMO participants are precisely what get appropriate government action to pacify the protesters, but this is disputed by some other research. Some SMS/SMOS have been successful in consistently using non-violent strategies and tactics (Della Porta, 2006; Roberts & Ash, 2009; Sharp & Paulson, 2005; Shock, 2015).

Most SMOS are usually composed mainly of participants (or friends or relatives of people) who suffer from the situation (e.g., denial of human rights, civil rights, basic necessities, or common amenities) they seek to change in their society (e.g., women, the poor, factory workers, farmers, racial-ethnic minorities, university students, the elderly, the disabled, teachers/professors, etc.). However, some SMOs have been comprised mainly of altruists working for a separate (non-member) *target of benefits* (Gamson, 1990), comprised by a category of people not included much or at all in in the SM/SMO (such as, slaves, the mentally or physically disabled, children, etc.). Further, SMOs are not organizations of the government or the business sector (or the household/family sector). *Initially, all participants in SMOs are volunteers,* although larger, more enduring, and more effective SMOs tend to develop over time at least a small cadre of part-time or full-time leaders/organizers, who receive at least subsistence incomes via the SMO/SM. *In the longer term, the large majority of participants in SMOs are unpaid volunteers.* Hence, the impacts of SMOs are part of the total impact of MAS—the focus of this paper.

Given all of the foregoing, it is no surprise that SMOs and larger SMs have achieved many remarkable, sociocultural changes in their own societies in the past 200 or so years, and often in global human society. Lofland (1996, pp. 348–353) has usefully suggested a rather comprehensive set of analytical categories/types of possible SMO effects, outcomes, or impacts: (a) changes in governments, laws, policies, policy systems; (b) winning acceptance; (c) new or enlarged movement establishment; (d) new items of mainstream culture; (e) shifts in norms, cultural images and symbols; (f) changes in the interaction order; (g) the shape of strata (socio-economic status) structures; (h) cultural clarification and affirmation; (i) entertainment and spectacle; (j) violence and tyranny; (k) scholarly trade (academic pursuits/activities studying the SMO/SM); and (l) models for later SMOs.

The early and exemplary, systematic, comparative research by Gamson (1990, first edition published in 1975) studied a *random* sample of fifty-three American SMOs (termed *challenging groups*), all of them MAS (usually national MAS), examining published documents about each SMO, using a standardized set of questions that investigated various hypotheses and theories about the causes of SMO impact/effectiveness. From among the (much-later published) set of twelve potential kinds of impact listed and discussed by Lofland (1996), as above, Gamson (1990, pp. 28–29) independently chose versions of (a) and (b) above, which he called *new advantages* and *acceptance.*

One very striking result of Gamson's (1990) research was that *fully 49% of the randomly sampled SMOs from this period of U.S. history achieved new advantages, as an indicator of SMO success.* Virtually no one would have expected this high success rate in advance. Given his random sampling of SMOs, these results can be generalized to all (over 1,500) major, American SMOs in this time period of 145 years. Most of the book explores the significance of various factors of resource mobilization and organizational structure/process associated with the two measures of SMO success. But *the central result for present purposes is* the great average effectiveness of SMOs as a type of MA *in a democracy like the USA over the time period studied.*

There is a huge research literature, including histories, that documents the impact of the many human rights-based SMOs in the USA and elsewhere in democratic nations. The twenty-nine chapters of the social movements handbook edited by Snow, Soule, and Kriesi (2004) give a brief overview of this literature. Chapters 24 to 29 and their references document the impacts of such major SMS as the labor, women's/feminist, environmental, peace/antiwar, ethnic/nationalist, and various religious movements. Careful reading of social and institutional history in industrial and post-industrial nations, for instance, clearly indicates that the life situations, life opportunities, and general life satisfactions have been substantially greater for factory workers, women, consumers of the environment, conscientious objectors, a variety of racial-ethnic groups, and members of many minority/fringe religions since relevant SMS and SMOs have been active in seeking such outcomes. Less clear is that the improvements have been the direct results of SM/SMO activity, but research such as Gamson's (1990) and studies of many single SMS/SMOs suggest that *these social movements and associations have indeed had a significant long-term impact.*

In addition to trying to understand participation in and the dynamics of SMS/SMOs (see (Smith, Stebbins, & Grotz, 2016, Chap. 24), many scholars have studied the outcomes-consequences of specific, single SMS/SMOs since about 1950. In many cases, the researchers involved have concluded that the SM/SMO has had some significant, positive impact on the targets of benefits—the kinds of people who were to be helped. Some examples are the books on types of SMS/SMOs such as the following:

- the abolitionist/anti-slavery SM (Aptheker, 1989; Blackburn, 2011; Drescher, 2009; Jonas, 2007);
- the black civil rights SM in America (Andrews, 1997; Blumberg, 1991; Jonas, 2007; McAdam, 1982; Morris, 1984; Olzak & Ryo, 2007);
- the various historical phases of the women's rights SM (Banaszak, 1996; Ferree & Hess, 1995; Ferree & Martin, 1995; Minkoff, 1995; Nikkhah & Zhairinia, 2011; Reagin, 1995);
- the labor/trade union SM (Galenson, 1994; Gall, Wilkinson, & Hurd, 2012; Goldfield, 1989; Mihlar, 1999);
- the environmental SM in America and Europe (Dalton, 1994; Dunlap & Mertig, 1992; Imam, 2009; Markham, 2008; McFarland, 1976;
- the anti-war/peace SM (Carsten, 1982; Chatfield & Kleidman, 1992; Hall, 2011);

HISTORICAL IMPACTS OF VOLUNTARY ASSOCIATIONS

- the neighborhood and community organizing SM (Atlas, 2010; Berry, Portney, & Thomson, 1993; J. Fisher, 1984; R. Fisher, 1994; Fung, 2006; M. Gittel, 1980; R. Gittel, & Vidal, 1998; Herring et al., 1998; King, 2004; Lancourt, 1979; McKenzie, 1994; Milofsky, 1988; Sirianni & Friedland, 2001; Smock, 2004; M. E. Warren, 2001).
- the various university student SMS (Abdalla, 2008; Hayden, 2012; Smith, 1973a);
- the disability rights SM (Gold, 2010; Haskins & Stifle, 1979; Lane, 1992; Potok, 2002; Shapiro, 1993);
- the elderly and senior rights SM (Amenta, 1998; Beito, 2000; Powell, Williamson, & Branco, 1996).
- the children's rights SM (Hawes, 1991);
- the abortion rights and anti-abortion SMS (Blanchard, 1994);
- the nativist/anti-immigrant SM in the USA and elsewhere (Knobel, 1996);
- the animal rights SM (Finsen & Finsen, 1994; Jasper & Nelkin, 1992).
- the SM to ban landmines (Faulkner, 2007).

The foregoing, brief list only *scratches the surface* in three different ways:

(a) Most of the documents cited above are books about American (USA) SMS/SMOS, making their citation here easier for the author who is American;
(b) The list of types of SMS/SMOS above is very incomplete, given the many other, usually less well studied, SMS/SMOS in the huge research literature from other times and all other places (e.g., Anderson & Herr, 2007; Snow et al., 2013);
(c) The documents cited for SM/SMO types listed are also incredibly incomplete.

The Google Scholar website (scholar.google.com; accessed December 2, 2017) listed 4,650,000 hits/documents when searched for the keywords *social movement*. The two recent three-volume encyclopedias cited just above at (b) collectively give the best, current global overview of the full range of SMS/SMOS in prior human history, as well as showing how they work and ideas about why they succeed or fail.

Since the 1980s, many other scholars have studied comparatively the outcomes, consequences, and impacts of SMS/SMOS, following the path-breaking research of Gamson (1990 [1975]). I can only mention here a few documents that seem to be the best summaries of this SM/SMO outcomes/consequences/impacts literature. Amenta et al. (2010) conclude their review of the political consequences of SMS/SMOS as follows:

"In the past decade, there has been extensive research on the political consequences of movements. The biggest and best-studied movements have been shown to be politically influential in various ways, and movement protest is especially influential in helping to set policy agendas" (of government legislatures and executive agencies). Amenta et al. (2010, p. 293) present a table of the impact (influence) results from their comparative content analysis study of nine main SM types, based on articles in five relevant, high-quality journals published in 2001–2009. For seven of the nine SMs, the authors found evidence of moderate or strong influence. For five less well studied, non-US SMs (names not reported), they found such evidence for all five SMs. Hence, overall, they found moderate or strong influence for twelve SMs out of fourteen examined. The two SMs with weak or no influence were the nativist/white supremacist SM and the antiwar SM. The main positive outcome types were single or multiple policy changes by the government.

An earlier review by Burstein and Linton (2002, p. 381) of research on political organizations in general, including SMs/SMOs, stated similarly as follows: "Everyone who studies democratic politics agrees that political parties, interest groups, and social movement organizations (SMOs) strongly influence public policy" in a variety of ways (specified). The authors also stated (p. 382), "They seem indispensable [as organizational forms] to democratic policy making; no democratic polity in the modern world is without them...."

Many other scholars have reached roughly similar conclusions regarding substantial impact of SMOs on average (Frey, Dietz, & Kalof, 1992; Gillion, 2013; Giugni, 1998, 2004; Giugni, McAdam, & Tilly, 1999; Meyer, 2007, 2014; Meyer, Jenness, & Ingram, 2005; Minkoff, 1997; Skrentny, 2004; Snow, Soule, & Kriesi, 2004, Part V; Tilly, 2004; Uba, 2009). Most of Gamson's (1990) conclusions about the internal, mobilizing factors affecting success/failure of SMs/SMOs have been confirmed, but there are still major theoretical and methodological difficulties and nuances of interpretation (Giugni, 1998, 2004; Jenkins & Klandermans, 1995; Meyer, 2007). In particular, other scholars have argued for the significant, sometimes substantial, effects of external factors, such as public opinion, culture, opportunity, and political party support (Amenta et al., 2010; Banaszak, 1996). Meyer and Whittier (1994) also showed that the influence of another SM could be significant. Feldmann (2016) suggest a variety of useful tactics the SMOs could use to improve their success and impact, based on his own extensive experience.

HISTORICAL IMPACTS OF VOLUNTARY ASSOCIATIONS   41

7   *Political Interest Groups or Pressure Groups as MAS*

(Political) Interest Groups (IGs), or Pressure Groups, are usually political advocacy MAs that systematically use *conventional* political means to achieve their goals (Smith, Stebbins, & Dover, 2006, p. 122), as contrasted with SMOs, which by definition use *unconventional* means, such as protest or even violence, to achieve their goals. (Note: I usually omit the implied adjective *political* to avoid having the abbreviation being *PIGs*, with negative connotations in English.) However, IGs can also be for-profit businesses. In authoritarian or totalitarian societies, IGs usually do not exist to any significant extent, since there is no democratic political system (i.e., legislatures, executive branch agencies, court system) on which to bring to bear external MA (IG) influences. However, some underground/secret IGs often exist, as DVAs, even in dictatorships (see Smith, 2018a, 2018b). As for SMS/SMOS, effective civil liberties are an essential aspect of democracy, if IGs are to have significant impact (Bresler, 2004, Bresler et al., 2016; Inazu, 2012; McWhirter, 1994; Scherr, 1989).

IGs have been of significant interest to political scientists since the start of the discipline early in the late 19th and early 20th centuries, but scientific interest waxes and wanes over periods of decades, not necessarily in relation to their impacts on events in countries studied (Baumgartner & Leech, 1998). The latter book performs a valuable review of the literature on IGs through the late 20th century, with various suggestions for improving future research on IGs. An important overall conclusion is that the IGs are often important influences on government, especially at the national level in democracies, but also at the next level down (states, provinces, regions). Hudson and Hudson (2013) argue and document that *"membership-based organizations shape America"* (in the title of their book). Berry has authored a series of books reviewing IG research (such as, Berry, 1997; Berry & Wilcox, 2008), reaching balanced conclusions about the powerful influence of businesses and business IGs (e.g., Clawson, Neustadtl, & Scott, 1992; Givel & Glantz, 2001), but seeing other types of IGs as also powerful. Berry has also written reviews of the role of nonprofits as IGs (Berry, with Arons, 2005).

Hojnacki et al. (2012) perform a broad review of the IG research literature more recently for the USA, mainly. They discuss three main types of theory that have guided research on IGs: normative theory, formal theory, and empirical theory. Among many substantive conclusions reached, these authors concluded (p. 9.14) that, "although entrenched political power in Washington favors the status quo, when advocates for policy change do succeed—an outcome that often occurs only after years of trying—policy tends to change significantly." The authors also concluded (p. 9.14) that, "between 1960 and 1990 liberal citizen groups shifted the congressional agenda toward more post-material issues." The newer literature on IGs (p. 9.15) focuses more on "interest group influence or the tactics and strategies that organizations employ in their efforts to achieve it," with more attention to "the context in which organizations operate to affect public policy." Many other books (e.g., Baumgartner & Leech, 1998; Van Deth, 1999) and thousands of journal articles for over a hundred years have studied IGs, and there are many textbooks and review books (e.g., Cigler, Loomis, & Nownes, 2015; Goldstein, 1999; Lowery & Brasher, 2004; Walker, 1983). The handbook edited by Maisel and Berry (2010) is an especially useful review of IG research.

Burstein and Linton (2002) wrote an important summary article and literature review comparing the *impacts* of political parties, interest groups, and SMOs. Based on a literature review of IG influence in some major journals of sociology and political science for the period 1990–2000, their conclusions (p. 381) include the following:

> "[P]olitical organizations [including IGs] affect policy no more than half the time; parties and nonparty organizations affect policy about equally often; there is some evidence that organizational activities that respond to electoral concerns of elected officials are especially likely to have an impact." Rauch (1995) has argued that the large numbers of conflicting IGs in the USA leads to a kind of stalemate, or *demosclerosis*, such that it is difficult for any specific IG to have much political influence and impact.
>
> But the tendency for negative or null results *not* to be published suggests that the actual frequency of successful influence is much less than that. The book by Baumgartner et al. (2009) similarly suggests that lobbying by IGs is much less successful than often assumed or asserted. Studying ninety-eight issues, 60% of recent lobbying campaigns were unable to change policies, even though millions of dollars were spent in the effort. The congressional system in Washington has a huge status quo bias, and resources explain very little of the success vs. failure outcomes of lobbying. But lobbying essentially represents conservative/elite interests, so change is usually slow, when present.
>
> Aside from considerable *status quo* bias by most government agencies in most nations, even strongly democratic ones (Barber, 1984), there is also a strong tendency for IGs with better resources/finances to have more influence than less well-resourced IGs. Schlozman, Verba, and Brady (2012) review much research demonstrating that the *unheavenly chorus* of elite IGs has a dominant influence on legislation and government

agencies. Some say, with substantial accuracy, "money buys access, and even influence."

Langbein (1986) used multiple regression analysis to show that PAC campaign contributions affected significantly the number of minutes that US Congressional Representatives spent with organized IGs in a typical workweek (with other variables controlled statistically). Yackee and Yackee (2006) studied rulemaking by the federal bureaucracy in the US over the period 1994–2001 regarding thirty bureaucratic rules and about 1700 comments by IGs. They found (p. 128) that, "business commenters [as IGs], but not nonbusiness commenters, hold important influence over the content of final rules." Similarly, Fordham and McKeown (2003) studied Congressional floor votes for the period 1979–1990 on foreign trade issues using multiple regression analysis. They found that (p. 519), "Economic interests account for a substantial portion of the variance in all cases, and models that also include other explanatory variables are highly accurate in estimating floor votes [outcomes]." However, as noted earlier, Berry and Wilcox (2008) argue clearly for the influence of other types of IGs, even including citizen and charitable nonprofits.

Evans (1996) studied influences on US Congressional committee decisions, with the criterion variable being IGs getting what they wanted from committees on their policy preferences in regard to two complex bills. Although IGs did not always get their desired outcomes, having more IG committee staff substantially led to greater IG success. Golden (1998) studied rule-making for eleven rules at three major US government agencies, finding the following:

> "a dearth of citizen commenters, the predominance of participation by business interests, and the presence of issue networks, and the absence of any discernable bias in whose voices get heard." Walker (1983) showed earlier that IG origins and maintenance, and hence success, depend especially on group leaders attracting non-member funding to maintain operations.
>
> Dur and de Bievre (2007b), introducing a special journal issue on IG influence, discuss many factors that complicate IG influence estimates in research. Various authors have discussed the methodology of such measurement (e.g., Dur, 2008; Kluver, 2009).
>
> Various authors dispute the apparent significance of IG influences on public policy, and the dominance of IG resources/finances as a key factor in IG success. Although there has been an advocacy group (IG) *explosion* (rapid growth in numbers) in the past several decades in America and Europe (Berry & Wilcox, 2008, Chap. 2), Gerber (1999) argued that IG

finances/spending do not always translate into much influence on public policy, based on various data sources. R. Smith (1995) reviewed mainly US IG research, concluding that the research presents a mixed picture of IG outcomes, rather than strong support for widespread IG influence on public policy. European IG research finds a similar mixed picture of IG outcomes: Dur and de Bievre (2007a, p. 79) reviewed European IG research, concluding that, "although [MAS] have gained access to policy-makers, they have largely failed to shift policy outcomes in their favour."

8   *Political Parties as MAS*

Smith, Stebbins, and Dover (2006, p. 177) define a political party as an, "association whose primary goal is to select and help elect a slate of candidates for governmental office. Once in power, the party has, as an additional goal, governance of the jurisdiction on which the election centered. Broadly, the goal of political parties is to gain and retain a monopoly on political power." Political parties are a form of MA that occurs mainly in multi-party democracies that have had electoral politics sometime in the past two centuries and/or the present one (Katz, & Crotty, 2005). However, parties also exist in one-party states that are not democracies, nearly always being authoritarian or totalitarian dictatorships. Prior versions of political parties, as in ancient Greece (Calhoun, 1970), were very limited in size and importance (Dahl, 1998 Chap. 2). Social scientists have been studying parties (always meaning *political* parties here) intensively for the past 100 years or so. Michels (1962 [1915]) wrote an early book treatment of parties, emphasizing oligarchical tendencies in their leadership. By now, there are many hundreds of books and thousands of articles on parties, attempting to understand how they work and their impact.

Strom (1990, p. 565) usefully distinguished three different models of competitive party behavior, or goals: "the vote-seeking party, the office-seeking party, and the policy-seeking party," developing a unified theory of party types/ models. Going into further depth and complexity, Gunther and Diamond (2003) develop a new typology of "species" of parties, with "genuses" (as clusters of similar species) based on three criteria:

(1)   the nature of the party's organization (thick/thin, elite-based or mass-based, etc.);
(2)   the programmatic orientation of the party (ideological, particularistic-clientele-oriented, etc.); and
(3)   tolerant and pluralistic (or democratic) versus proto-hegemonic (or anti-system).

Aldrich (1995) wrote a book-length discussion and analysis of why parties came into existence in the USA (see also, Leonard, 2002). He argues that parties were devised to deal with three deep problems of democracy: (a) mobilizing voters to vote in elections; (b) regulating access to public office; and (c) establishing majorities to accomplish policy goals once in office, and maintaining such majorities. Aldrich argues that in the 1960s, parties in the USA became more candidate-centered, essentially beholden to specific candidates. Aldrich (2011) reprises his earlier book, adding some current/recent context. Cohen (2003, p. 808) reported four empirical studies of individuals that showed that, "attitudes toward a social policy depended almost exclusively upon the stated position of one's political party," even though "participants denied having been influenced by their political group." This and similar research suggests that parties have substantial impacts on their constituents and/or that constituents with congruent ideologies are drawn to appropriate parties. Recent handbooks and textbooks deal in depth with parties and elections, in which parties play an important role (e.g., Dalton & Klingemann, 2009; Hershey, 2014; Katz & Crotty, 2005; Leighley, 2012; Leonard, 2002; Maisel & Berry, 2010). The most comprehensive overview of parties in every nation is Lansford (2015).

Some authors have tackled the question of party impacts globally, usually finding significant or even substantial impacts on the nations involved (e.g., Castles, 1982). A simple recognition of the impacts of historically important political parties confirms this generalization, at least in the most relevant cases: the Bolshevik party in the Soviet Union (Brovkin, 1994), the Nazi Party in Hitler's Germany (McDonough, 2003), and the Chinese Communist Party under Mao (Zheng, 2010), to name a few. But all of these examples are parties in one-party states and dictatorships, not parties in multi-party nations, showing that the party form of organization as a pseudo-MA (i.e., without true voluntariness and democracy/civil liberties), can have important meaning and impact, even without genuine electoral politics and democracy.

But in this section, the focus is mainly on multi-party states/nations. Historically, experts, including political leaders, have been writing about parties for two centuries (e.g., Silbey, 2002; Van Buren, 2015). Some books review the historical development and present state of parties in the USA and other Western nations (e.g., Adkins, 2008; Chandra, 2017; Cole & Deighan, 2012; Reichley, 2000). Many books illustrate how parties in various nations promote, represent, and seek to develop government policies that foster various political ideologies, which is one major aspect of parties as noted above by Aldrich (1995, 2011) and given extended treatment in the handbook by Freeden, Sargent, and Stears (2015). Hybel (2012) argues that ideologies have been important ways that humans have sought to cluster themselves for 1700 years, even before parties, and more crucially since parties arose about 200 years ago.

For instance, nationalism has been a popular ideological theme of parties in many nations, as contrasted with an international/multinational theme (e.g., Breuilly, 2013; Comaroff & Stearn, 1995; Herb & Kaplan, 2008). Parties with right-wing, conservative ideologies have also often appeared in national polities worldwide (e.g., Bob, 2012; Schain, Zolberg, & Hossey, 2002; Williams, 2006), often related to nationalist ideologies (e.g., Rock, 1995). Of course, the left also has had many parties, in the USA and elsewhere (e.g., Jeffreys-Jones, 2013; Katsourides, 2016). Religious parties are also frequent, as noted in the next section of this article, and are often right-wing or nationalist (e.g., Kalyvas, 1996; Preston, 2004). There are Islamist parties as well as parties with Christian or other world religions as ideological themes (Aboul-Einein, 2013; Ayoob, 2007; Springer, 2009). In colonial nations, there have often been freedom-seeking parties, which can be seen as a special type of nationalism (e.g., Odendaal, 2013). In many countries, parties arise that are based on socio-political movements (SMOs) other than the ones above (Schlozman, 2015). Environmental/ecological parties have been common in Europe in recent decades (Barnett, 2001; Garner & Jaggard, 2011). Some authors have written about *global parties*, a new concept, based on widespread ideological themes shared by various nations (e.g., Sehm-Patomaki & Ulvila, 2007).

Multinational comparative studies, based on literature reviews, of the impact of parties on legislation generally find significant impact of parties in the relevant nations. The survey by Burstein and Linton (2002) is most impressive, though dated now. They analyzed the results of assessing the impact of political organizations (parties, interest groups, social movement organizations/SMOs) as studied in fifty-three articles from three top US sociology and three top political science journals for the period 1990–2000 (p. 389). There were 230 countries involved in the fifty-three articles, but 73% of these were about the USA, and all dealt with developed countries (p. 390). Overall, 60% of the political organizations had some impact, but only 20% had significant and substantial policy importance (p. 394). About 12% of parties studied had impacts with significant and substantial policy importance, as contrasted with about 29% of interest groups and SMOs (p. 394). Thus, political MAs do have an impact in many nations, but less impact than might be expected. Also, the parties had a statistically significant and substantial impact less than half as often than other political MAs, suggesting that the parties studied are much less efficacious than interest groups and SMOs. Resources of the organizations generally had an effect on impact 65% of the time, not surprisingly (p. 398).

HISTORICAL IMPACTS OF VOLUNTARY ASSOCIATIONS

A related multinational study of the impact of parties on government policy was reported by Knill, Debus, and Heichel (2010). The dataset used "includes information on the number of [pro-] environmental policies adopted in 18 OECD countries at four points in time between 1970 and 2000. The results show that not only international integration, economic development and problem pressure, but also aspects of party politics, influence the number of policies adopted." These results held up under a number of control variables examined jointly. The two multinational studies above are quite convincing with a quantitative approach to party influence on government policies. Other similar or related quantitative studies lend further support to the significant impact of parties on policies across various nations in recent decades.

However, there are countervailing kinds of evidence of the weakening of party influences on policy that also need to be taken into account here, especially in post-modern (post-industrial) countries like the USA. Simply put, the strength of party influences on individuals seems to have been waning in the past few decades in many nations, especially in advanced industrial and post-industrial democracies. For instance, Wattenberg (2009) argued with data that American elections 1952–1996 have become more candidate centered, rather than ideology- or party-centered. A key kind of evidence has been the inability of parties to mobilize more than half of the eligible electorate in presidential elections. Dalton and Wattenberg (2002) further support this thesis for twenty OECD nations in the later 20th century, finding individual party identities weakening/eroding in nearly all advanced industrial democracies. Dalton (2013) continues to make this case, but some authors argue the contrary (Boix, 1998). The truth is likely that, while party identities are weakening in postmodern nations, they still have some significant influence in such nations, and even more in agrarian and modern/industrial nations. The handbook edited by Maisel & Berry (2010) is an especially useful review of political party research.

9   *Democratization MAs*

This type of global impact MAs specializes in attempting to promote democracy (especially effective civil liberties and fair contested national elections) in a society or nation, usually by peaceful/nonviolent means, but sometimes by violent means, especially prior to about 1950.

Socio-political revolutions, guerrilla campaigns, and underground resistance campaigns (above) may or may not lead to democratic (or more democratic) outcomes. We all know the democratic outcome of the American Revolution, but many socio-political revolutions and guerrilla campaigns have simply replaced one kind of autocracy with another, one kind of autocrat with another, as in the Russian, Chinese, Nicaraguan, and Zimbabwean revolutions, to name only a few examples (Gilbert, 1991; Martin, 1981; Skocpol, 1979).

Democracy, as rule or governance by the people, is a very old idea, but very *recent* historically in its extensive implementation in human societies, mainly occurring in the past two or three centuries (Tilly, 2007, p. 9). However, in various 18th- and 19th-century nations with some legal form of democracy, "Parliaments were often no match for a monarch" in practice (Dahl, 1998, p. 23). According to Dahl (1998, p. 8), democracy in the sense of full or male suffrage (the right to vote in national elections), began only about 1860, and rose gradually from one nation in 1860 to sixty-five nations by 1990. There was a leap from thirty-seven nations in 1980 to sixty-five nations in 1990. Huntington (1991) has referred to this rapid growth in the numbers of democratic nations in the last-quarter of the 20th century "the third wave of democratization."

When the USA was founded and its Constitution ratified by 1790 by constitutional conventions of all thirteen original colonies, the USA was *not* very much of a democracy. To participate in the early US democracy, one had to be an adult, male, own land, and not be a slave (Vile, 2012). Those restrictions left out the vast majority of the citizens/population of the USA, as the *first new nation* (Lipset, 1963; Tilly, 2007, p. 9). Over the course of the next 200 years or so, MAS in the form of specific SMS/SMOs have pushed the American Congress to broaden greatly the US democracy in terms of all those constraints noted. Dahl (1998, p. 23) noted that, "As late as 1832 in Great Britain the right to vote extended to only 5 percent of the population over age 20," in spite of enfranchisement laws. Dahl's Figure 1 (1998, p. 24) shows that even by 1914, only 30% of the population over 20 could vote.

Thousands of publications in the past 2500 years have tried to define democracy in an objective manner, applicable to any society or nation-state anywhere and anytime.

Dahl (1972) wrote an influential book defining *democracy*, which he preferred to call *polyarchy*. In Table 10.1 (p. 203) he summarized his theory of polyarchy (democracy) in seven principles. Coppedge and Reinicke (1990) constructed an index of various empirical indicators of polyarchy. Vanhanen (2003) created a data archive with various indicators of democracy for all existing nations from 1810 to 2002.

J. Fisher (2013, p. 8) summarizes Dahl (1972) and March and Olsen (1995) in defining democracy as having four requirements or dimensions: "political opposition, public participation, and law-based civil liberty," plus "a democratic political culture."

J. Fisher (2013, p. 9) listed seven special advantages of living in a democracy.

It has long been clear that various freedoms and civil liberties are prerequisites for democracy (e.g., Bresler, 2004; Inazu, 2012; McWhirter, 1994; Scherr, 1989). That necessity is why the Bill of Rights was attached officially to the US Constitution as equally binding Amendments. Freedom House, an NPO based in New York City, makes annual ratings on many indicators of political rights and civil liberties, which are crucial aspects of democracy in many definitions (Tilly, 2007, p. 1).

In his magisterial book on democracy, democratization, de-democratization, and their interdependence, with the simpler title, *Democracy*, Tilly (2007, Chap. 2) showed that the indicators of democracy and overall indices vary greatly not only across nations, which is common knowledge, but also vary greatly across historical time for many nations. In Chapter 8, Tilly gives his answers to many key questions about why these variations in democracy across places and times have occurred.

Several important research projects have investigated the political, economic, and social structural factors associated with the presence of democracy in large sets of nations. We will cite only a few of these as examples (see also other studies listed at Vanhanen's website: www.services.fsd.uta.fi).

Przeworski et al. (2000, p. 7) studied many nations with the "aim to assess the effects of political regimes on material well-being." Regimes were classified into a dichotomy: democracies and dictatorships (p. 10) using published "historical observations of 141 countries between 1950 (or the year of independence) and 1990" (p. 14). Conclusions included the following:

- "[P]oor people are much more likely to be ruled by dictators" (p. 269).
- "Political regimes have no impact on the growth of total income when countries are observed across the entire spectrum of conditions" (p. 270).
- "[L]ives under dictatorships are grim and short" (p. 271).

In another multi-nation study, Inglehart and Welzel (2005) analyzed data from four waves of the World Values Survey for over eighty nations, along with other data. Their results (pp. 6–9) show quite conclusively that *post-modern, self-expression values (vs. industrial or agrarian society survival values) when widespread in a nation's population predict and explain the development of democracy in the many nations studied.* The authors state (pp. 5–6) that, "the inherently emancipative nature of self-expression values makes a democracy increasingly likely to emerge; indeed, beyond a certain point it becomes increasingly difficult to *avoid* democratization."

When the two waves of the World Values Surveys, before and after the "Third Wave of democratization" in the late 20th century were examined, the "levels of self-expression values had a stronger impact on levels of democracy after the Third Wave" than the level of liberal democracy before the Third Wave had on self-expression values (Inglehart & Welzel, 2005, p. 9). Further, self-expression values clearly differentiated nations with effective democracies from weaker, more nominal democracies (p. 9).

Teorell (2010, p. 116) studied 165 countries around the world regarding determinants of regime change 1972–2006, finding that violent collective actions like riots, strikes (at times) or domestic conflicts (e.g., civil wars) had no significant relationship to democratization. However, "peaceful demonstrations were a positive trigger of democratization during the third wave." Teorell (p. 144) also found that among dictatorships, "multiparty autocracies during the third wave were in and of themselves more prone to democratize than one-party dictatorships."

Inglehart and Welzel (2005) did not gather direct measures of participation in MAS, interest groups, SMOS, or other collectivities potentially involved in the democratization process (p. 224). However, they argue (p. 211) that, "democratization takes place through collective action, such as mass demonstrations, liberation campaigns, and bargaining processes at the elite level...." The authors suggest that case studies of specific nations are needed to investigate such issues (ibid.).

J. Fisher's (2013) book describes such case studies of the impact of NPOS, especially MAS, as *democratizing NPOS* in South Africa, Tajikistan, and Argentina. She argues (p. 4) that, "the growth of civil society [including especially MAS] and democratization is a demonstrable phenomenon throughout the world," citing five supporting references. A variety of other scholars have made the same case for active MAS, or civil society more generally (with an emphasis on MAS), as causal factors in democratization and/or the maintenance of effective democracies (Dahl, 1998, p. 98; Diamond, 1999, Chap. 6, 2007; Edwards, 2011, Chaps. 1, 8, and 30; Florini, 2000; Gamwell, 1984; Kupermus, 1999; Perez-Diaz, 1993; J. Smith, 2008; Walzer, 1983; M. E. Warren, 2001).

However, MAS, including purportedly democracy-seeking revolutionary MAS, do not *guarantee* democratic outcomes, as noted in the first paragraph of this Section D, #3. The review article by Fung (2003) and review book by Tilly (2007) make this point clear. Much depends on the personality/character of the key revolutionary leader(s). For instance, George Washington was offered the position of king of the new USA, but, having deeply democratic values and a certain *democratic personality* (see Smith, 1995), he turned down that offer and settled for being the first US president, exiting that role after two terms, when he did not really have to do so. The situation/regime outcomes for the ostensibly democratic, MA-based revolutions in Zimbabwe, Nicaragua, China, Cuba, and many other nations have been long-term totalitarian dictatorships.

It is an interesting fact of the past 100 years of world history that so many nations resulting from *ostensibly* democracy-seeking SMS/SMOs and resulting successful political regime changes have led to long-term totalitarian dictatorships with names like *The People's Democratic Republic of....* Obviously, the *appearance* of democracy, if only in a false name, is a valued commodity for autocrats/dictators, where *kingdom* or *empire* appealed more to autocrats/dictators for many prior centuries and millennia.

10   *Religious MAs and Movements*

Contemporary sociologists of religion have very general definitions of religion, seeking to fit all kinds of religion throughout human history. For instance, Johnstone (1992, p. 14) defined religion as, "a system of beliefs and practices by which a group of people interprets and responds to what they feel is sacred, and, usually, supernatural as well." More recently, Bellah (2011, p. xiv) defined religion as, "a system of symbols that, when enacted by human beings, establishes powerful, pervasive, and long-lasting moods and motivations that make sense in terms an idea of a general order of existence." Note that the latter definition does not beg the question by including the central, nearly synonymous term, *sacred*, nor the term *supernatural.*

The treatment of religion here is social scientific, rather than theological. The roots of religion in human societies are contested. Anthropologists and sociologists have argued that religion has universal *functions* or benefits for societies, for local congregations, or for national or international religious bodies as MAs (Emerson, Mirola, & Monahan, 2010). For most of humanity's 200,000-year history on earth, religion was an integral part of human society and culture, as a *cultural universal*, with no known exceptions (Brown, 1991, p. 139). However, the evidence for that statement is very recent and inferential, based on anthropological field work in the past 200 years or so with various pre-contact, hunting-gathering nomadic tribes (see Lowie, 1970; Webster, 1908). Initially, religious occupational specialists were shamans, though the tribal chief could also have a special role as head of religious matters and rituals. For most of human existence, religion was *not* really a distinct part of life nor a special entity, such as an MA or other institution/agency: religion was part of being human in some specific society. According to Brown (1991, p. 139), based on massive evidence from prior independent fieldwork by hundreds of trained anthropologists, the universal aspects of religion are the following: supernatural beliefs, practice of magic, theories of fortune and misfortune, practice of divination, performance of rituals, and belief in a unified world-view, that "is part of their supernatural and mythical beliefs" (p. 139). Some religious activities were accompanied by music.

In the past few decades, social scientific religion scholars have asked broader questions about the history and development of religions, rather than mainly describing and cataloging them and their main features from the earliest times. Cox (2017) discusses this new approach, eschewing the older term *primitive* and preferring the more neutral label *indigenous*. More sophisticated books on the anthropology and history of religion have appeared recently, and have done more refined analyses of the history and development of indigenous religions (e.g., Kansal, 2012; Malefijt, 1989; Menzies, 2016). Some such books have provocative titles, such as *The invention of God* (Römer & Geuss, 2015), *A history of God* (Armstrong, 2004), and *The evolution of God* (Wright, 2009), focusing on analytical changes in conceptions of God/gods and the supernatural, usually involving new varieties of prior religions and new or altered religious MAs.

Increasingly, scholars in the past century have begun to view independent religions as organizations, not just as an aspect of human culture, especially in agrarian societies and more complex modern or post-modern societies (e.g., Demerath et al., 1998). This organizational, or more accurately, *associational* (MA) approach to religion has been led by Protestant Western scholars (e.g., Robertson, 1966). Scherer (1972) long ago argued that religions, especially local units, are usually MAs. Cnaan and Curtis (2013) have more recently shown local congregations to be MAs (see also, Chaves, 2012; Cnaan et al., 2016). In modern multi-religious societies/nations, there are often many denominations of Christianity (e.g., Greeley, 1972), various movements/varieties of Islam (e.g., Rubin, 2009), and types of Buddhism (e.g., Queen, 1996; Snelling, 1998), among other world religions.

Contrary to earlier anthropological, sociological, and psychological explanations for indigenous and also borrowed (non-native) religions, some scholars in the past twenty years have explored evolutionary and behavior genetic bases for human religions and religious faith (e.g., Thomson & Aukofer, 2011). In a magisterial *magnum opus*, Bellah (2011) makes a convincing case both for the evolution of religions in human societies and simultaneously for the evolution of behavior genetics supporting and interacting with the societal evolutionary processes. More popular/general readership books in the same vein write of the *faith instinct* (Wade, 2009) and *born to believe* (Newberg & Waldman, 2006), both based on solid genetic evidence and evolutionary theory.

Given these underpinnings, it is not hard to understand in general terms how we arrived at the present, highly multi-religious versions of many (but far from all) contemporary nations and the highly multi-religious entire world system. Large cities arose in various countries as part of developed civilizations about 5000 years ago (in Sumer, Egypt, China, Greece, etc.), resulting from the agrarian revolution in some economic systems (that is, more sophisticated and productive agriculture; Nolan & Lenski, 2006). These cities, and both trade and migration to them, led to new religious ideas and theologies being brought from other places or invented (e.g., Dutt, 2012; Gray, 2016; Montgomery, 2012; Stark, 1997). Many of these led to new religious MAs, and some of these led to the various major world religions extant today (Juergensmeyer, 2011; Prothero, 2011; Rubin, 2009; Stark, 1997, 2012; Woods, 2008).

Sometimes new religions in history have (sooner or later) become *state* religions in one or more societies/countries, by definition integrated with a national government, but usually also having a separate MA with formal members. An alternative label for this situation is to term the society/nation a *theocracy*. The head of state is usually the titular head of the state religion, and may hold the most power, but there is usually also a (different) top clergyperson in charge of the national religious MA and religious events, such as coronations, royal marriages, and state funerals. For instance, in England or the UK more recently, the sovereign (reigning king or queen) is the titular head of the Church of England (Anglican Church), but the Archbishop of Canterbury is the clerical/religious head. State churches have been dying out or diminishing in power in the 20th century, especially in modern, multi-religious nations (Littell, 1962).

In modern and post-modern nations with substantial democracy, civil liberties, and especially full freedom of religion, denominations, as national or sub-national, independent, religious MAs have proliferated over time, as in the USA (e.g., Mead & Hill, 2001). Many nations now have directories or encyclopedias of active religions (usually meaning denominations) within their borders (e.g., Melton et al., 2009). Religion researchers have studied in detail the development of large numbers of independent religious denominations in various nations (e.g., Woods, 2008), as MAs, especially the USA (e.g., Finke & Stark, 2005).

In addition to large numbers of independent religious MAs in modern democratic nations, as rather established denominations, there are also many recently formed MAs formally termed *new religions*, but also termed pejoratively *cults or sects* (e.g., Clarke, 2006; Hammer & Rothstein, 2012; Lewis, 2008). By contrast, many scholars have remarked on and documented to some extent the decline of religion/religious MAs and participation in them in the West (e.g., Taylor, 2007). For many people, especially the university-educated in modern Western nations, atheism seems to be ascendant (Bullivant & Ruse, 2016). However, religion and religious MAs remain a major global force among most of the world's population, who are not university educated and not living in Western nations (Berger, 1999; Micklethwait & Wooldridge, 2010; Thomas, 2005; Toft, Philpott, & Shaw, 2011).

A secular aspect of the importance/impact of religious MAs in recent global society is the link between religion and electoral politics, especially political parties in multi-party polities in the past two centuries or so. As discussed in section E. #8 of this paper, mass political parties have arisen very recently in human history, accompanying the development of genuine democracies since about 1776, especially in the 1800s and early 1900s (Tilly, 2007). Admittedly, the extension of voting rights to former slaves, women, and non-landowners has taken until the 20th century in nearly all nations (Dahl, 1998, Chapter 2). The first democracies in the 18th and 19th centuries in European nations and the USA, with widespread elections of the top leader(s), only admitted free adult males, usually with wealth, as legitimate voters.

When multi-party systems arose in electoral democracies in the 19th century, often one party at least had some clear ties to traditional religion in the nation. There are many books analyzing the role of religion in US politics, both recently and for the past two centuries, all finding significant religious effects (e.g., Fowler et al., 2013; Wald & Calhoun-Brown, 2006; Wilcox & Robinson, 2010; Williams, 2012). In Europe, the same situation has prevailed for two centuries—significant impact of religion on politics (Burleigh, 2007; Depkat & Martschukat, 2013; Kalyvas, 1996; Preston, 2004). Other world regions show the same pattern of religious influence on electoral politics, when present, such as in Latin America (Azaransky, 2013; Cleary & Stewart-Gambino, 1996; Levine, 2012; Lowy, 1996). Research on democratic elections also shows the impact of religious MA affiliation or participation on voting by individuals (Esmer & Pettersson, 2007; Green, 2010).

Another secular aspect of the impact of religion occurs at the individual level. Much research shows that more religious people tend to get more involved in religious volunteering, but also more involved in secular formal volunteering (e.g., Cnaan et al., 2016). This relationship has been found in survey research in many nations (e.g., Bennett, 2015; Lam, 2002, 2006; Ruiter & De Graaf, 2010). This relationship gains importance when one examines the impacts of formal volunteering on the individual, most of which are positive (e.g., Smith, 2016b; Wilson et al., 2016), including better health, greater longevity, more positive affect/well-being, etc. The Edwards (2011) handbook shows that both MAs in general (Chap. 5) and religion/religious MAs (Chap. 21) contribute significantly to civil society worldwide. Other survey data indicates that religious faith is associated with more happiness in life (Brooks, 2008, pp. 93, 197).

HISTORICAL IMPACTS OF VOLUNTARY ASSOCIATIONS

(a)   The Dark Side of Religion

Now a skeptic may ask, so what? How else do all these religious MAs around the globe and their participant religious volunteers matter, with electoral politics, ideology, and potential prayers aside? Religious violence comes to mind immediately, given the events of the past century and present one. But religion-related violence goes back millennia, not just a century or two, let alone a decade or two. Given powerful human genes for aggression and thus for violence (e.g., Wilson, 2004, Chap. 5), humans, especially human males, find nearly endless reasons/excuses for violent individual and collective behavior, including religious differences. Religion-based wars go back millennia, including the Christian Crusades of course (Armstrong, 2000) and the Roman Catholic Church's medieval Inquisition that murdered tens of thousands of alleged heretics (Lambert, 1992; Moore, 1977 [1994]; Perez, 2005). The handbook edited by Juergensmeyer, Kitts, and Jerryson (2015) covers some distant historical examples of religion-based violence as well as more recent and familiar examples, with appropriate analyses of important details of when religious violence has occurred and why. Fortunately, Pinker (2012) has demonstrated, with global quantitative data, that over recent centuries and millennia, human violence, especially collective violence, has been declining, including religious violence.

Nonetheless, there is still, and long has been, much religious violence in absolute terms, especially when the purported peacefulness and kindness professed by most world religions is taken into account (Avalos, 2005; Ellerbe, 1995). Pretty clearly, the theological and moral proscriptions against violence, including religion-based violence, do not deter all that much of such behavior/events globally. Armstrong (2014) discusses how originally warrior-based, violent religions arising about three to five thousand years ago transitioned into very different peace/kindness-based world religions that we know today. The connection of religion to violence, she argues, comes from the fact that humans, especially males, are often aggressive and violence prone, not from the essence of religion itself. There is no space here to review the litany of even major religious violence events in the past 100 years, but suffice it to mention the Nazi holocaust directed at European Jews, 1939–1945 (Friedlander, 2008), so-called *ethnic-cleansing* in the Balkans, which had a religious component (Carmichael, 2002), and the genocides in Africa, which also had religious as well as ethnic aspects (Straus, 2015).

There are many academic books that review and analyze religious violence since about 1990 around the world, but especially in Europe (e.g., Avalos, 2005; Juergensmeyer, 2009; Lewis, 2011). Ellerbe (1995) attributed much religious violence to the theology and structure of the Christian Church over two millennia. Many other authors point to and seek to analyze the etiology of the recent spate of religious violence by Islamic militants (e.g., Esposito, 2003; Juergensmeyer, 2003; Rennie & Tite, 2008; Rubin, 2009; Springer, 2009; Sproul & Saleeb, 2003). Stern (2004) interviewed Christian, Jewish, and Islamic militants regarding their motivations for killing in the name of their God. She found that in all three religions such killings were often the result of opportunistic leaders who used religious motivations and arguments/justifications to recruit marginal, disenfranchised youth with little to lose. The specific religion appealed to was not crucial. There is also significant violence linked to *new* religious movements/new religions as MAs, as well as to varieties of long-established world religions (Lewis, 2011).

As another example of long-term ideological shifts among world religions/ religious MAs, in an earlier book Armstrong (2000) showed how the theme/ ideology of fundamentalism arose over centuries and millennia in various major world religions/religious MAs. These ideological/theological shifts had significant impacts on the level of religious violence subsequently, including in wars.

11 *Scientific-Learned MAs*

These MAs generally represent academics and researchers in scientific and scholarly fields, covering mainly basic science, but also increasingly applied science. In a real sense, such MAs are professional MAs, but they are different from other professional MAs: Storer (1966, p. 16) stated that science differed from other major professions because "it is a 'non-service' profession—a profession that does not serve the needs of laymen directly." This is the conceptual basis for treating such MAs separately here.

Scientific-learned societies/MAs sprang up in late medieval/pre-industrial times by providing reliable knowledge as a basis for economic and technological innovations and sustainable development/SD (McClellan, 1985; Ornstein, 1963 [1913]). Such scientific/scholarly associations also were linked to research universities in this late medieval/pre-industrial period in Europe (de Ridder-Symoens, 1992) and North America (Hall, 2006). Such universities in later centuries have become aspects of technological and social innovation as crucial factors in sustainable economic development in industrial and post-industrial nations, especially affecting the rise of knowledge-based professions that dominate modern societies (Krause, 1996; Smith, 1997b).

Sociologists have identified several basic institutions of all human societies, such as the economy, polity, kinship and a few others, but science is not usually among these (Nolan & Lenski, 2006). Science as a basic institution of human society has undergone huge growth since 1600, and especially since about 1800

(Marks, 1984). Science is far more than research and discovery; science is also a social system, as Storer (1966) has discussed long ago. He pointed out that scientific MAs are important parts of that social system, as *integrative mechanisms* (p. 148), with a key role in providing dissemination and recognition for scientific advances and individual scientists making them. Storer (1966) writes of such MAs at different territorial levels and also different levels of generality versus specificity of focus: At the most general level of focus and the national territorial level of the USA, he mentions (p. 148) the American Association for the Advancement of Science (AAAS), and also the institutionally related American Association of University Professors (AAUP). But he goes on to note there are large national scientific MAs for various academic disciplines (e.g., biology; p. 149), and "smaller, specialty-oriented groups" (p. 162).

Schofer (2003) has performed seminal historical and quantitative research on the "global institutionalization of geological science, 1800–1990" (p. 730). Utilizing an alternative theory of scientific development, *sociological institutionalism*, he demonstrates how the "spread of professional geological associations" (p. 730) in the past two centuries has been crucial to the establishment of geology as a globally recognized academic discipline in the major universities worldwide. Hence, scientific MAs not only are integral to science for individual scientists, but are also central to the spread and recognition of entire academic disciplines and, by extension, smaller specialty fields.

The history and sociology of science is a special interdisciplinary field in itself, studied by many historians and scientists of various academic disciplines (e.g., Bucchi, 2004; Marks, 1984; Merton, 1973; Pyenson & Sheets-Pyenson, 2000; Rehbock, 2001; Storer, 1966; White, 1993).

Scientific-learned MAs tend to have annual (or less frequent) conferences at which scientific-learned papers are given and discussed, but also often sponsor one or more academic journals (e.g., Backhouse & Fontaine, 2010; Cattell, 2016; McClellan, 1985; Ornstein, 1963 [1913]). Texts on IGs often have a chapter on scientific MAs.

Scientific-learned MAs' most important impact is on the active scientists in the world, especially basic researchers (versus applied researchers). Scientific MAs are integrative mechanisms for dissemination and recognition, as noted in fourth paragraph above. Such MAs can also have a major impact on certain political issues where scientific research and conclusions are crucial, such as tobacco use, global warming, and the like. But the most important global and historical impacts of MAs are via motivating and encouraging individual scientists and in fostering the global advance of science. Fortunately, Pinker (2018) has just sent to press a magisterial book reviewing the long-term impacts and benefits of science for society.

12 *Economic-Support MAS*

By *economic-support MAS* I refer to MAS that, while *not* profit-seeking businesses of any kind, nonetheless support businesses, occupations, and the economic sector of society. Primary examples, as sub-types, are trade and business MAS (TBAS), trade/labor unions, farmers' MAS, professional MAS, scientific and learned MAS, and other occupational MAS. All of these types of economic-support MAS have had, especially since about 1800, and continue to have, important impacts, both economic and political, in contemporary nations worldwide. I treat scientific & learned MAS separately as subsection #11 above, because, although related to one's occupation, and hence professional MAS, they are a special case in not being direct service professions (Storer, 1966, p. 16).

(a)   Trade and Business MAS/TBAS

Unlike most other MAS, which have individual persons as members (Smith, 2017a), these TBAS usually have business firms as organizational/collective members. Collectively, they have a major positive economic impact on specific types of businesses or economic activities, including through their involvement as IGs in many cases (e.g., Assael, 1968; Becker, 1990; Bonnett, 1956; Coleman & Grant, 1988; Givel & Glantz, 2001; Goldsmith, 2002; Hakonson, 2013; Harner, 2012; Spillman, 2012). Texts on IGs often have a chapter on TBAS, as did the Palgrave handbook (Saitgalina et al., 2016) of volunteering and MAS. Knoke (1993) gave an overview of USA trade associations, based on national survey sample data. He was able to shed light quantitatively on TBA membership incentives.

(b)   Trade/Labor Union MAS

Such union MAS are the most widespread kind of economic support MAS in industrial nations, and are found in nearly every contemporary nation. The handbook by Gall, Wilkinson, and Hurd (2012) provides a solid overview of global research on unions. Martin (2008) performed a very useful study of which resources help unions to be successful at union organizing. As Galenson (1994) shows, unions have been in a general decline in recent decades with the global progression from industrial to post-industrial societies (see also Goldfield, 1989, on the USA). Mihlar (1999) shows that union-related right to work laws improve average wages in many nations, contrary to a positive impact of unions. But Smith (2000: 204) notes, "For instance, unions tend to raise their members' average wages locally compared to non-unionized workers in the same localities and industries (Estey, 1981, p. 134; Hirsch & Addison, 1986, p. 153). Estey (1981, p. 136) finds that unions hasten technological change

HISTORICAL IMPACTS OF VOLUNTARY ASSOCIATIONS 59

and raise overall firm efficiency (p. 137), while reducing the scope of management (especially personalized) decision-making (p. 135). Thus, there is substantial global evidence of the positive economic impact of unions on members' wages."

(c)   Farmers' MAS

These MAS have two distinct sub-types, with members who are either (i) farm owners or (ii) farm workers who are not also farm owners. The extensive but older bibliography on farmers' organizations (MAS, mainly) by Morrison (1970) suggests the breadth of US research on these MAS nearly fifty years ago, for the earlier historical period when farmers and farming were more important politically and economically in the USA (other relevant examples include Bruns, 2011; Fite, 1981; Stahura, 1999). Texts on IGS often have a chapter on farmers' MAS.

Of the two types of farmers' MAS noted, the impact of (usually poor) farm workers' MAS has been weakest of all economic-support MAS, even when the MAS are transnational (Borras Jr, Edelman, & Kay, 2008). However, Farm owners' MAS have often had major impacts both in politics and economics, especially before 1950 in the USA, but continuing to the present for certain crop types. Campbell (1962) discussed at length the political and economic impact of the Farm Bureau (a nonprofit association, although begun by the US government Agriculture Department) in 1933–1940. Givel and Glantz (2001) show the strong impact of the tobacco lobby, including the Tobacco Institute [a TBA], specific major tobacco companies, and tobacco farm owner MAS, on US state legislatures. The International Tobacco Growers Association unites tobacco farm owners from many nations and influences tobacco policy and legislation in many nations. The British Medical Association [a professional-scientific MA] (1986) report, *Smoking Out the Barons*, describes their fairly successful campaign to reduce tobacco use in the UK, with great opposition from tobacco companies and tobacco farm owner MAS.

(d)   Professional MAS

These MAS represent usually well-established professions, like teaching/education, medicine, nursing, pharmacy, management, public administration, social work, law, engineering, etc. (Abbott, 1988). There are thousands of such MAS, with national and state or local scope (e.g., Gokturk et al., 2017). The MAS are often concerned with licensing, continuing education, upholding professional standards, and the like (e.g., Abbott, 1988; Higgins, 1988; Krause, 1996; Selinger, 2000). Texts on IGS often have a chapter on professional MAS. In addition to advancing these important and societally vital occupations integrally based on extensive formal education, professional MAs are often also significant influences on political processes and legislation, as shown by the previously cited references. Professional associations initially help build, establish, and spread professions and academic fields (Greenwood, Suddaby, & Hinings, 2002; Schofer, 2003).

13   *Social Innovation and Sustainable Development* MAs

Academics who study social innovation too often ignore the role of volunteering and voluntary associations as important sources of social innovation (cf., de Wit et al., 2017). A recent and thoughtful definition of *social innovation,* based on an extensive literature review, is the following (The Young Foundation, 2012, p. 18): "new solutions (products, services, models, markets, processes, etc.) that simultaneously meet a social need and lead to new or improved capabilities and better use of assets and resources." Other authors add the idea that social innovations need to potentially "improve either the quality or the quantity of life" (Pol & Ville, 2009, p. 881), which also seems like a useful definitional factor, excluding innovations "that have detrimental effects on society or the environment" (de Wit et al., 2017, p. 3).

Sustainable development (abbreviated as *SD*) refers to the socio-economic development of a society or nation-state that is enduring in the longer term, taking account of environmental limitations, sustainable livelihoods, and human well-being, in addition to temporary socio-economic development and growth (Hopwood, Mellor, & O'Brien, 2005; Redclift, 1987). A recent concept in development studies, originating in the late 1980s (Redclift, 2005), there has been huge debate from the beginning about what SD means and how it can be achieved, if at all (Lele, 1991; Redclift, 1987). The handbook on SD by Redclift and Springett (2015) provides the best recent overview of the issues and themes involved.

The basic research and theoretical question of this section is, "Does the current set of approaches to SD pay sufficient attention to research and theory about MAs/associations and volunteering as popular participation in SD." I offer as *negative* evidence the fact that none of the main areas/topics treated in the recent Redclift and Springett (2015) supposedly comprehensive handbook on SD deals sufficiently with such popular participation. But there are also some signs that SD scholars pay some attention to popular participation (Bell & Morse, 2008). In this section, I propose to describe briefly the extensive prior research showing how important MAs, in particular, are in providing social inventions and then later social innovations related to SD. The first time some new social solution or idea is proposed, it is a social *invention.* When that

HISTORICAL IMPACTS OF VOLUNTARY ASSOCIATIONS 61

solution or idea is copied, adopted, and diffused in the larger population, it becomes a social *innovation*.

(a)   Four Global Associational Revolutions in Human History
        Affecting SD

Innovation scholars often ignore the fact that MAs/associations themselves as a category of human groups are themselves a social invention and often subsequently a social innovation. Only recently has the history of MAs in human societies become clear in scholarly writings. I summarized the global history of grassroots (local) MAs first in my (Smith, 1997b) article, citing major prior books that are relevant (such as Bradfield, 1973; Ellis & Noyes, 1990; Kloppenborg & Wilson, 1996; Ross, 1976; Waltzing, 1895; Webster, 1908) and some key articles (Anderson, 1973; Conradi, 1905; Hartson, 1911; Schlesinger, 1944). Two Smith (2010b, 2010c) chapters also review briefly the history of MAs, and their major theoretical characteristics, as contrasted with paid-staff-based nonprofit agencies or voluntary agencies (Smith, 2015b, 2017a). More recently, a multi-authored general review of the history of associations was published with extensive references (Harris et al., 2016).

In press at the time of writing is my article (Smith, 2018d) describing *four major global associational revolutions* in human history. These four associational revolutions have been summarized as follows (Smith, Stebbins, & Grotz, 2016, p. 1213):

> Here is the correct historical sequence of the four global associational revolutions. See Smith [2018d] for more on the underlying sea change in the economic system that [first] precipitated each revolution of interest.
>
> [i] [FIRST] The Original-Horticultural (O-H) Associational Revolution (about 10,000 years ago, *c.* 8000 BCE; Smith 1997[b]).
> [ii] [SECOND] The Agrarian and Urban (A-U) Associational Revolution (about 5000 years ago, circa 3000 BCE; Smith 1997[b]);
> [iii] [THIRD] The Industrialization-Modernization (I-M) Associational Revolution (about 1800 CE; Smith 1972a);
> [iv] [FOURTH] The Service-Information-Technology (SIT) Associational Revolution (circa 1950 CE; Salamon 1994, 1995; Smith [2018d]).

Each of these associational revolutions involved an initial social invention that became a social innovation, and also affected SD globally. The First Associational Revolution had a SD effect in preliterate societies (tiny nomadic tribes of 30–70 people) mainly on quality of life for the members of the social and sometimes religious clubs involved (Bradfield, 1973; Lowie, 1948, Chap. 13; Simmons, 1945; Webster, 1908). But the Second Associational Revolution had a SD effect in the urban areas (towns, cities) of ancient agrarian societies, especially on economic and occupational SD, fostering sundry urban occupations (Lambert, 1891; Waltzing, 1895; Weisberg, 1967). But such associations also had a SD effect on quality of life, since ancient guilds provided social and welfare services for members and their families, especially in the case of members' death. In ancient agrarian societies, there were also SD effects on quality of life via religious and political aspects of associations (Calhoun, 1970; Kloppenborg & Wilson, 1996). Some ancient societies also had early academic/scholarly associations, which contributed to SD by providing educational and scientific underpinnings for future economic activity and SD (Chroust, 1967; Conradi, 1905). Most ancient agrarian societies also had various religious associations that contributed to SD quality of life in religious beliefs and activities (Duchesne, 1912; Harland, 2003; Ross, 1976; Shafer, 1991).

In the centuries between the Second and Third Associational Revolutions, especially in the pre-industrial societies in medieval times about 1000–1700 CE, a variety of associations flourished in many European societies and North America (Hartson, 1911; Smith, 1997b). For instance, occupational guilds flourished in Europe in this period (Epstein, 1991). The Epstein and Prak book (2008) on medieval guilds as associations specifically emphasizes the social innovations involved in SD during 1400–1800. Gadd and Wallis (2006) also describe how guilds in the period 900–1900 have contributed to social innovation and SD.

The Industrial Revolution and its accompanying *Organizational Revolution* (Boulding, 1953) led to the Third Associational Revolution in all industrializing societies/nations, with such industrialization and modernization still continuing in many contemporary nations (Inglehart, 1997; Inglehart and Welzel, 2005; Inkeles & Smith, 1974). Boulding's (1953) brilliant book on the organizational revolution first emphasized this critical change in industrial societies, with hugely more businesses of many kinds and also many more government agencies and units, as social innovations affecting SD. However, Smith (1972a) was the first to describe and provide empirical data demonstrating the Third Associational Revolution. Salamon (1994, 1995) much later wrote about an associational revolution, but was historically incorrect in describing the Fourth such revolution, *not* the first one as he implied (as was Casey, 2015).

I wrote recently (Smith, 2018d), "These economic and social structural changes of the Industrial Revolution as a massive economic social innovation fostered a wide variety of new types of associations affecting SD, including

HISTORICAL IMPACTS OF VOLUNTARY ASSOCIATIONS 63

associations for leisure/recreation/sports/trade[/labor] unions, professional/occupational associations, new types of religious associations/congregations, scientific[/scholarly] societies, political parties/clubs, social movement organizations, and eventually self-help groups like Alcoholics Anonymous."

(b)   Key Social Innovations Fostering SD in Global Associational History

Taking the USA as a well-studied example, there have been several systematic social innovations present in the history of associational development since 1800. The first major one was probably the early development in the 19th century of three territorial levels of associations (national, state, and local) as influenced by national association-organizers (Skocpol, Ganz, & Munson, 2000). This innovation had a profound impact on the speed and breadth of development of associations in the USA for the next two centuries (Ellis & Noyes, 1990; Hall, 2006; Hammack, 1998; Neem, 2008; Schlesinger, 1944). This growth is sketched in Gamm and Putnam (1999) with reliable quantitative data for 1840–1940 for US cities and towns. There are many books dealing with the historical growth of specific purposive types of associations in the USA and elsewhere—women's associations (Scott, 1992), amateur arts associations (Blair, 1994), trade/labor unions (Galenson, 1994; Pelling, 1963), employers' associations (Bonnett, 1956), fraternal/social associations (Schmidt, 1980), men's service clubs (Charles, 1993), religious associations/churches (Finke & Stark, 2005), political parties (Reichley, 2000).

A related key social innovation in the development of associations in the USA was specifically the growth of *national* associations in the later 19th and 20th centuries, as described for higher education national associations by Hawkins (1992). Also significant was the social innovation of forming associations with collective or *organizational members*, rather than only individual persons as members. Associations of businesses as collective members were among the first examples of this special structural type of association in the USA, as reviewed by Bonnett (1956) for employers' associations. Trade and business associations (TBAS) are now familiar association types worldwide (Saitgalina et al., 2016).

A further systematic social innovation regarding the growth of associations in the USA and elsewhere, particularly in Western Europe in the later 19th and 20th centuries, was *trans-national and international associations*. Commonly termed *INGOs*, international non-governmental organizations date back perhaps two millennia (Davies, 2013, p. 20), with various early transnational religious orders being nearly a thousand years old (such as the Roman Catholic Order of St. John dating to AD/CE 1099). Modern INGOs of many types began to arise in the 1760s and thereafter (Davies, 2013, p. 24), often with charitable, social change, or economic goals, thus serving SD. INGO growth in numbers has been rapid in the late 19th and 20th centuries, with a variety of significant multinational and sometimes global impacts.

In addition to INGOs, at the trans-national level there are also many associations of governments, as collective/organizational members. I (Smith, 2015b) wrote, in summary (quoted with permission):

> At the global level, it can be argued that INGOs, as international Associations, have been global moderating influences, often ameliorating or resolving transnational conflicts, as well as building world culture, for the past century and more (Boli & Thomas, 1999). Even the many Inter-Governmental Organizations (IGOs) of the world, like the United Nations and the Organization of African Unity, are in fact Associations of governments as organizational members. These IGOs play key roles in peace and war, providing multinational forums for discussion and delivering certain key services as public goods, including fostering economic and social development. But there are also noxious and harmful INGOs like Al Qaeda that are active on an international scale. Like all other types of human groups (families, businesses, governments), Associations mainly do good and useful things, but also can do very harmful things at any geographic level.

I also wrote recently (Smith, 2018d), "The Fourth global associational revolution began about 1950, as certain nations became post-industrial, service-information-technology societies. New technologies like the computer, mobile phones, and the Internet spurred personal inter-communication and facilitated the growth of associations, especially national and international associations, but also local associations." Casey (2015), Ellis and Noyes (1990), Hall (2006), Harris et al. (2016), O'Neill (2002), and many others describe the range and variety of these associations that are part of the Fourth Associational Revolution in the USA. Many books also describe contemporary associations and volunteering in the other world regions and nations—Butcher (2012) for Mexico, Dalton (1994) for Western Europe, Dunlap & Mertig (1992) for the USA, Guo et al. (2012) and Handy et al. (2007) for India, McCarthy et al. (1992) global, Obadare (2014) for Africa, Pekkanen (2006) for Japan, Sanborn and Portocarrero (2006) for South America, and J. Smith (1993) for Europe. Smith, Moldavanova, and Krasynska (2017) covers the former Soviet Republics, and Wang (2011) covers China, while cyber/internet associations are an entirely new development (see Adams & Smith, 2008; Rheingold, 1994).

HISTORICAL IMPACTS OF VOLUNTARY ASSOCIATIONS 65

(c)   Global Impacts of Associations Affecting SD
In my chapter for the *International encyclopedia of social and behavioral sciences*, 2nd edition (Smith, 2015b), I wrote the following conclusions (quoted with permission):

> Recent research (e.g., Smith 2000: Chap. 9; Smith [2016b; Wilson et al., 2016]) shows clearly that member volunteering in Associations leads usually to many positive outcomes for participants. Such positive impacts include better mental and physical health, greater happiness and satisfaction, better social relationships and more social capital, political empowerment and influence in many cases, greater information and certain skills, and sometimes economic and occupational advancement.
>
> Looking at the larger community, many Associations have clear and positive impacts on local problems and issues [relevant to SD]. For instance, the national Association in Bangladesh with the acronym BRAC has been extremely successful in helping poor people there and elsewhere in the Global South with their own economic development and poverty issues (Smillie, 2009). This is not an isolated instance, as Fisher (1993; see also 1998) shows convincingly. Local development GAs and Supra-local, grassroots-support organizations are one key to sustainable development in Third World nations, she argues. Even when considering related issues in the Global South, Associations have important roles to play, such as in helping urban migrants adjust in big cities (e.g., Little, 1965). However, GAs may also have negative impacts on their members or on their local communities. Delinquent juvenile gangs [and terrorist groups] are one of many possible examples.

(d)   Associations and Volunteering as Public Participation in SD
In spite of the established fact that associations and volunteering as public participation contribute significantly to SD (Beito, 2000; Eberly & Streeter, 2002; Esman & Uphoff, 1984; Fisher, 1993, 1998, 2013; Gunn, 2004; Handy et al., 2007; Skocpol, 1992; Smillie, 2009; Smith, Baldwin, & Chittick, 1980; Smith & Elkin, 1980; Stout, 2010), SD scholars and planners spend insufficient time or effort building such factors into their theories, plans, indicators, and implementation. However, Redclift's (1987) early book on SD devoted Chapter 7 to discussing how environmental movement associations have contributed substantially to SD in regard to environmental management. According to Bell and Morse (2008, p. 22), summarizing the Bellagio Principles regarding SD, broad participation is required for appropriate SD, and (p. 30) the United Nations "working list of indicators of social development" includes "Strengthening the

Role of Major Groups." There are also occasional papers or reports that emphasize public participation in regard to one or another element of SD (Pahl & Jones, 2012).

Most importantly, perhaps, there is a strand of SD data gathering that emphasizes a kind of public participation termed *Rural Appraisal* (Chambers, 1995), and more importantly a related practice termed *Participatory Rural Appraisal* (*PRA*), both of which seem promising, but are not widely used. In his Table 1, Chambers (p. 9) summarized PRA, developed in the late 1980s and 1990s, as involving NGOS (associations), with its predominant mode being "Facilitating, participatory" and its "ideal objectives" being "Empowerment of local people" while having as "longer-term outcomes" both "Sustainable local action and institution[s]." Chambers further notes (p. 14) that PRA is "participatory," allowing and encouraging local rural people in developing nations "to be dominant, to determine much of the agenda" [of SD], and "to plan." This approach reverses the usual approach of most planners and implementers of SD, which has been top-down and authoritarian, giving local people little real say in forming the SD agenda and plans.

Chambers further argues with case examples that PRA is substantially effective in bringing about SD (1995, pp. 29–35). He proposes (p. 36) that for local participatory approaches to be successful there needs to be "greater confidence and professionalism in rural NGOS" [associations]. Chambers sees PRA as involving a paradigm shift in SD approaches, usually favored mainly by "NGOS; Government field organizations; and universities and training institutes." Associations have led the way in accepting and using PRA/participatory approaches to SD, not surprisingly.

Chandra (2010, p. 286) quotes the following as one definition of participation, consistent with involvement of associations and volunteering, as advocated here:

> "'With regard to rural development ... participation includes people's involvement in decision-making processes, in implementing programmes, their sharing in the benefits of development programmes and their involvement in efforts to evaluate such programmes.'" A variety of references illustrates the value of PRA. It is important also to recognize the potential or latent effort/work represented by associations globally. Smith (2014c) is one of very few scholars to estimate the total number of associations in the world as a whole. Based on a variety of empirical research by many scholars from sundry nations, he estimates there are about seven associations per 1000 population in the world as a whole.

HISTORICAL IMPACTS OF VOLUNTARY ASSOCIATIONS

Quoting from that Smith (2014c) paper (with permission of the author):

> Based on the current global population of about 7 billion, and the esti-
> mated global prevalence of seven Associations per-thousand-population,
> the present author estimates *that there are about 56 million Associations
> worldwide at present.* Of these, about 49 million (roughly 90%) are GAs
> [local, grassroots associations]. Some 7 million additional NPGs [non-
> profit groups] are PSNPOs [paid-staff nonprofit organizations], mainly
> Nonprofit Agencies. An estimated one billion people now are members
> of one or more Associations, and even more will be members sometime
> during their lifetime.

This raises the issue of the economic value of all the volunteering done in the
world, both *formal* volunteering in associations and volunteer programs, and
informal volunteering (voluntary interpersonal helping/service) done outside
any formal group. In Smith (2014c), the following conclusion is stated:

> Salamon, Sokolowski, and Haddock (2011) estimated by extrapolation
> from their own research on 40+ nations that there are roughly 1 billion
> volunteers worldwide (971 million). This is likely to be an underestimate,
> because nearly all socialized humans do some *informal* volunteering in
> any given year. [...] *The results indicate about 971 million people volunteer
> in a typical year worldwide (p. 22), with 36% being formal volunteers and
> 64% being informal volunteers.* The estimated total economic value of
> this volunteering in 2005 was USD$ 1.348 trillion (p. 23). This number was
> equivalent to the 7th largest economy in the world in that year. Another
> estimate yields the total value of USD$ 1.49 trillion, with more extensive
> extrapolation (p. 23, fn).

14   List/Typology of Major MA Purpose/Goal Subtypes

In another document (Smith, Stebbins, et al., 2016, pp. 90–125), I have identified and described the main activity/goal/purposive types of MAs comprehensively. While not discussing all of these types (p. 100) here, I have dealt at some
length with types 2, 3, 4, 5, and 6, which seem to have had the most impact on
human societies and history. A case could be made for discussing all of the
other types, but space constraints prevent me from doing so here, plus the fact
that their impact seems less on human societies and history.

The 10 key MA goal/purpose types identified are as follows, with an additional miscellaneous category (quoted with permission here from Smith,
Stebbins, & Grotz, 2016, p. 100):

The proposed *Tenfold Typology of Association Purposes* is as follows (with some example documents for the several MA sub-types *not* dealt with above, with an *):

1. *Philanthropic/Charity-Social Service-Health/Medical-Education Associations [e.g., Beito, 2000; Carter, 1961; Morgan, 2013; Newcomb & Wilson, 1966]
2. Political Influence-Advocacy-Rights Associations and Parties
3. Social Movement Organizations/Associations & Activism
4. Community Improvement-Protection-Economic Development-Poverty Alleviation Associations [e.g., J. Fisher, 1984; R. Fisher, 1994; Gittell, 1980; Lancourt, 1979]
5. Occupational-Economic Support Associations (farmers, factory workers [trade unions], white collar workers [employee-associations; unions], professionals, businesses-employers' associations)
6. Religious-Ideological-Morality Associations
7. *Self-Help-Support-Improvement-Personal Growth Associations [e.g., Borkman, 1999; Gartner & Riessman, 1984; Katz & Bender, 1990; Wuthnow, 1994]
8. *Sports-Recreational-Exercise Associations [e.g., Nichols, 2017; Rojek, Shaw, & Veal, 2006; Stebbins, 2002; Young, 2016]
9. *Arts-Music-Culture-Study Associations [e.g., Blair, 1994; Pierce, 2006; Slezak, 2000]
10. *Sociability-Conversation-Conviviality Associations [e.g., Charles, 1993; Kaufman, 2002; Ross, 1976]
11. *Other Associations (e.g., hobby-games-garden-plants-animals leisure associations; environmental-ecology-flora/fauna preservation associations, automobile-trailer-caravan-travel leisure associations; investment-financial management clubs; residential associations [monasteries, communes]; family concerns-planning-birthing-child rearing associations; infrastructure-support associations; deviant voluntary associations].

F   Conclusion

1   *Some of My Prior Relevant Conclusions about MAs*
In conclusion, I argue that the global historical and societal impact/influence of MAs, as the first and still most frequent type of NPO globally (Smith, 2014c), is far greater in contemporary and recent societies/nations worldwide than the

long-term impact of any other NPO analytical type, such as nonprofit agencies (voluntary agencies, or Volags), foundations, or social enterprises. I think most people, including voluntaristics scholars/academics (Smith, 2016a), are usually misled by thinking about MAs in far too narrow terms, as Scouts, Alcoholic Anonymous/AA, school and university clubs, or sports associations. The correct definition of an MA fits far more important types of MAs, reviewed here, that have brought about substantial and often enduring changes in specific societies, especially nation-states, since about 1800, and in the global human society as a whole.

In Smith (2015b), I wrote the following conclusions (quoted with permission):

> At the level of nations, [MAs] have often had a major impact throughout the Western nations and often in Eastern and Southern nations as well, both positive and negative (Smith, 1966, 1973a, 1974, 1997a, 1997c, 2000, Chapter 9; Smith & Elkin, 1980, 1981). As a beginning, political parties are [MAs], and have had vast importance and impacts in the politics of most modern nations, including one-party states. Some parties have brought freedoms, but others have brought oppressive dictatorships. Delving deeper, social movements and especially their component social movement organizations [SMOs] are [MAs] that have changed history worldwide in the past two centuries [Gamson, 1990; Giugni, McAdam, & Tilly, 1999; Tilly, 2004, 2007]. Social movement [MAs] have significantly helped the situations of slaves, farmers, laborers in factories, women, children, older people, racial-ethnic minorities, the disabled, gays and lesbians, and many other categories of historically disadvantaged people with special needs or problems (Gamson, 1990; Tilly, 2004). Associations have also been vital components and preservers of democracy in many nations (Fisher, 2013; Tilly, 2004, 2007; M. E. Warren, 2001), as manifestations of the participatory essence of civil society. Voluntary *Agencies* rarely play this vital role in civil society worldwide, lacking most participatory elements present in Associations.

In a more recent conclusion about the impacts of associations/MAs (Smith, 2017a), I stated the following (quoted with permission):

> [A]ssociations, especially social movement organizations, have the greatest long-term average impact on social progress in human history, sometimes referred to as *ethical evolution* [Broom, 2004; Kitcher, 2011]. When the impact of associations on communities and entire societies in human history is reviewed, the conclusion is that associations in general,

especially socio-political change-oriented associations, usually as components of social movements, have had massively greater impacts than [nonprofit] agencies. Such associations, *not* mainly nonprofit agencies or even governments, have been directly responsible for ending widespread slavery, gaining substantial rights for women and the handicapped, protecting gays and lesbians, and gaining rights for labor unions. Usually the associations with the greatest historical impact have been perceived generally as deviant and stigmatized when they first arose, because sociocultural change is usually strongly resisted in any society, such as the early anti-slavery or women's rights associations in various nations. Deviant voluntary *associations*, which seek goals that are generally rejected by their surrounding society, though quite rare, are much more frequent than deviant nonprofit *agencies*: It is easier and wiser to be deviant in one's leisure time than when one's job is at stake.

Comparing the sub-types of MAs reviewed in this article regarding relative, let alone absolute, levels of impact or influence is difficult, and probably impossible to do accurately. Most of the information/data is qualitative, and finding a common metric across the disparate MA sub-types is unlikely, if not impossible. So, what can we say, by way of summary, having reviewed various research literatures?

2 Several New Conclusions about MAs from This Review Paper

The following general conclusions from the evidence reviewed here seem reasonable:

(a) Each of the 13 main sub-types of MAs reviewed here can have and has had significant, sometimes substantial, impacts on their targets of influence in various societies/nation-states worldwide, especially since the Industrial and Organizational Revolutions, beginning circa 1800 CE (Boulding, 1953; Smith, 2018d).

(b) For any given institution/organization and/or issue as an influence target at a certain point/period in time, none of the MA sub-types studied can *guarantee* significant, let alone substantial, and enduring influence. The *status quo* is usually very hard to change, especially when the power-holders benefit greatly from it, but more feasible since about 1800 and the Industrial and Organizational Revolutions, occurring at different times in various countries 1800+ (Smith, 2018d). Even very powerful IGs, like the National Rifle Association in the USA (Davidson, 1993), sometimes fail, or at least have major setbacks, in their influence attempts.

HISTORICAL IMPACTS OF VOLUNTARY ASSOCIATIONS

(c) The current context of the national socio-political and military regime in a country at a given time or time period can have a marked effect on whether or not any kind of MA can change the situation in the way they desire (Bresler et al., 2016). Context sometimes is totally dominant. Significant political impact of MAS as discussed here is very rare, often impossible, in effective totalitarian regimes, and less hard but still difficult in authoritarian regimes (Allen, 1984; Bobbio, 1989; Friedrich & Brzezinski, 1956). The presence of significant democracy and civil liberties in a nation/society matters a great deal (Bresler, 2004; Bresler et al., 2016; Inazu, 2012; Scherr, 1989; Schofer & Longhofer, 2011; Smith & Shen, 2002; Tilly, 2004, 2007; M. E. Warren, 2001).

(d) As a considered qualitative judgment by the author, among all MA subtypes discussed here, Social Movement Organizations/SMOs seem most likely to have a significant influence on their targets of influence on average (that is, for all influence attempts) in contemporary nations worldwide, and to have such outcomes be enduring over decades or longer, but mainly in democratic or partially democratic societies with significant civil liberties (Bresler et al., 2016; M. E. Warren, 2001). Much qualitative and some quantitative empirical evidence supports this conclusion in many nations (Amenta et al., 2010; Burstein & Linton, 2002; Gamson, 1990; Giugni, 1998, 2004; Giugni, McAdam, & Tilly, 1999; Skrentny, 2004; Smith, 2018b; Tilly, 2004, 2007; Uba, 2009).

(e) Revolutionary, guerrilla, and civil war MAS are often successful in making a public statement of political resistance, but their long-term influence and success average in gaining power generally seems low on the whole. Only since about 1800 has this type of MA had a better, but still modest, average of successful political impact. The dominant political regime tends to use military and/or police force to smash them successfully in most cases, but less so in the past 100+ years. However, such deviant MAS have been much more successful on average since circa 1800 CE, especially in democratic societies and where effective civil liberties have been present (Bresler, 2004; Bresler et al., 2016; Inazu, 2012; M. E. Warren, 2001), rather than in authoritarian regimes (Allen, 1984; Bobbio, 1989; Friedrich & Brzezinski, 1956). In some countries, especially poor ones, such MAS are a popular way of expressing discontent, but with little longer-term success (Colburn, 1994). In some world regions (e.g., Latin America, Africa, the Middle East), such MAS are so common and so often unsuccessful as to be taken much less seriously than in world regions (or nations) where such MAS are uncommon (Colburn, 1994).

(f) Both Social Movement Organizations/SMOS as MAS and Revolutionary, guerrilla, and civil war MAS as two MA sub-types (#6 and #1 above in this list) tend to be more successful when supported by public opinion and/or by the opinion of political-business elites, let alone both, and when their focus is national rather than sub-national.

(g) MAS that have used disruptive, activist protest approaches have been especially successful since circa 1800 (Gillion, 2013; Piven, 2006; Piven & Cloward, 1979; Skrentny, 2004), but non-violent approaches have also worked at times, especially since 1900 (Engler & Engler, 2016; Roberts & Ash, 2009; Sharp & Paulson, 2005; Shock, 2015).

(h) Underground political resistance (UPR) MAS in foreign-army-occupied nations/societies, such as Nazi German armed occupation of various European nations just before or during WWII, can often have significant nuisance and publicity value against the occupying power, in some cases temporarily damaging a military or political regime. Longer term and summary impact is hard to assess accurately. The cumulative long-term impact of the French resistance as UPR MAS was (Schoenbrun, 1980, p. 374) "worth a hell of a lot of [armed services] divisions to us", when the Allied forces invaded France in Normandy on D-Day in 1944, according European commanding US General Bradley. However, in general, the UPR MAS in the many Nazi-occupied European nations were rarely truly successful in important ways, and even the French resistance MAS were largely unsuccessful in ending the Nazi occupation, both before and after D-Day (Gildea, 2015; Laska, 1985). De Gaulle fostered his own version of the myth of the French resistance, subsequently challenged and greatly revised (Gildea, 2015, pp. 445–481). The life expectancy of the French UPR MA resisters and their MAS was short and low, as elsewhere in Nazi-occupied Europe in WW II (Aubrac, 1993).

(i) Terrorist MAS seek to have political influence/impact and change the political system by use of public violence, aiming to generate widespread fear or even panic among the public of a target nation/society (e.g., Chalk, 2012; Combs & Slann, 2007; Schmid, 2013). Such MAS are of the same radical and violent nature as UPR MAS just discussed, and tend to have similar lack of long-term success on average. Indeed, the occupying Nazi Germans saw UPR MAS and their active members as simply terrorists (Gildea, 2015). Nonetheless, terrorist MA violence gains great notoriety in the mass media and arouses substantial fear in the population (e.g., Al Qaeda: Gunaratna, 2002; Wright, 2006), which is indeed a kind of widespread emotional impact in various affected countries.

Jackson et al. (2011, dust cover text) argued that, "Terrorism and the war on terror has affected virtually every aspect of modern life." That conclusion seems excessive, especially regarding terrorism itself. Most importantly, since terrorism itself (*not* including the *war on terror* or war against terrorism as essentially government responses to terrorism) is violence aimed at political change, the actual results of the intended political impact of terrorist MAs are not substantial on average (Chalk, 2012; Combs & Slann, 2007; Jackson, 2016).

(j) Because Hate MA aims are often vague and general (such as, "eliminate all the" Jews or black/colored people or foreigners), assessing impact is particularly difficult. But there is little doubt that some hate groups in some societies/nations have fostered hatred in the general population to some extent, challenged ideals of tolerance and fairness, and have harmed some targets of hate. However, an objective if qualitative assessment of Hate MAs must be that they and their actions rarely accomplish their broader stated aims of eliminating (killing or deporting) or imprisoning many or all of their targets of hate as a category. Hate MAs mainly talk hatred and spend much time training for and discussing an expected future race war or the overthrow of the federal government. Episodes of actual physical harm to targets of hatred tend to be few in numbers, and mass violence is very rare, although it does occur occasionally with great mass media notoriety.

The KKK in the USA, from the later 1800s down to the present, is one well-known US example of a Hate MA (Sims, 1996; Tucker, 1991). A related subtype of Hate MAs is Skinhead youth gangs in the USA (Hamm, 1994; Christensen, 1994). Since about 1960 in the USA, paramilitary militia MAs have been serious white racist hate groups (Abanes, 1996; Dees, 1997; Levitas, 2002; Stern, 1996). Abanes (1996) traced the ideological roots of American paramilitary militia MAs to white supremacist theories and the anti-Semitism of centuries ago.

Even strong hate groups usually do not endure long as specific MAs (versus the larger paramilitary movement and its ideology) in their influence, as they arouse significant opposition from the government and often the public if/when they commit violence and are identified as the perpetrators (Tucker, 1991). However, active and enduring hatred of some category of different others (by race, religion, national origin, gender preference, etc.) seems to be a recurring human characteristic, especially among the poor, less educated, and socially alienated.

(k) Deviant voluntary associations (DVAs) can often have substantial and enduring impacts on a society/nation, and even the larger world society.

Smith (2018b), in the forthcoming book, *Nonprofits daring to be different*, shows that there are three main categories of DVAs, noxious, dissenting, and eccentric (innocuous). I have discussed the impact of some *noxious* DVA subtypes here—(a) revolutionary, guerrilla war, and civil war MAS, (b) terrorist MAS, and (c) hate groups as MAS. I also discuss here two *dissenting* DVA subtypes—(a) underground political resistance MAS in foreign-army-occupied nations/societies, and (b) social movements/social movement organizations (SMOS) as MAS. Sometimes democratization MAS are also dissenting DVAs, as discussed here. I write little about *eccentric* DVAs (such as witches' covens or nudist MAS), because they have marginal impact, mainly on consenting members.

Among DVAs as MAS (Smith, 2018b), noxious DVAs such as the Nazi Party before and during World War II, often have substantial negative impacts on their own and neighboring societies (e.g., the holocaust and the European front in World War II). Eccentric DVAs have only minor effects, if any, on their larger society. But dissenting DVAs are generally SMOS, and often have significant and enduring substantial impacts on their own and on other societies, frequently contributing to societal and global *ethical evolution* (Broom, 2004; Kitcher, 2011).

In another forthcoming book on DVAs (Smith, 2018a), *A survey of deviant voluntary associations: Seeking 'method in their madness,'* I do informal content analysis of about 100 books on a variety of DVAs to develop a grounded theory of such MAS in recent history (mainly since 1800), selected as examples of 24 common sense categories of DVAs, developed by the author with Robert A. Stebbins: Citizen Militias/Survivalists/Paramilitary Groups; Communes/Intentional Communities, Religious and Secular; Coup d'Etat Groups; Cults/New Religions; Delinquent Gangs; Deviants' Activist Groups (prostitute self-help/activist) groups; Deviant Science MAS (UFO group [not a cult] and black magic MA); Gay or Lesbian MAS; Group Sex/Group Marriage/Swinging MAS; Guerrilla MAS; Hate Groups; Medieval Heresy MAS (Christian); Massacre/Doomsday MAS; Motorcycle Outlaw Gangs; Naturist/Nudist Groups; Political Parties (deviant); Revolutionary MAS; Religious Sects (deviant); Social Movement MAS (deviant); Terrorist MAS; Transvestite/Transsexual Groups; Underground Resistance Groups (WW II); Vigilante Groups (nongovernmental/informal justice groups); Witches' Covens.

(1) Political parties and interest groups (IGS) can be successful under special circumstances in democratic national regimes, but their impact success averages seem moderate to low on the whole (Baumgartner & Leech, 1998; Baumgartner et al., 2009; Berry & Wilcox, 2008; British Medical

Association, 1986; Burstein & Linton, 2002; Castles, 1982; Dur & de Bievre, 2007a, 2007b; Evans, 1996; Fordham & McKeown, 2003; Gerber, 1999; Golden, 1998; Hojnacki et al., 2012; Langbein, 1986; Schlozman, Verba, & Brady, 2012; R. Smith, 1995; Walker, 1983; Yackee & Yackee; 2006). Using a new theory of IG influence, Laumann and Knoke (1987, pp. 360–362) in a national quantitative study are able to show significant impacts of several IG types on events relating to health and energy in the USA. But such impact tends to be very low in dictatorships or missing, especially totalitarian ones (Allen, 1984; Bobbio, 1989; Friedrich & Brzezinski, 1956).

(m) Political parties and interest groups rarely take strong stands on the majority of possible issues or influence opportunities, owing to insufficient resources (including time), the multiplicity of contentious issues, variations in opinions, status quo biases, competing priorities, and the like. Such MAs tend to concentrate on national influence, with minor attention to state/province level issues, and very little if any focus on local levels (Dur & de Bievre, 2007a, 2007).

(n) Democratization MAs do not have a solid record of impact, partly because there are so many other, often more powerful, factors affecting the extent of democracy in a society/nation. Democratization MAs can be successful in highly educated, modern and post-modern nation-states, especially with much prior experience of democracy, but the transition can be very lengthy, taking decades or longer, with reversals occurring, often multiple times. Also, as noted earlier, Tilly (2007, Chap. 2) showed that the indicators of democracy and overall indices vary greatly not only across nations, but also vary greatly across historical time for many nations. From an 80-nation four-wave set of surveys, Inglehart and Welzel (2005, pp. 6–9) showed quite conclusively that *post-modern, self-expression values (vs. industrial or agrarian society survival values) when widespread in a nation's population predict and explain the development of democracy in the many nations studied.*

(o) Religious MAs, especially those that are well-established historically, can and often do have substantial prestige in some nation-states (especially in agrarian/pre-industrial nations, but much less so in post-modern/post-industrial nations), and those that have large memberships including some prominent people in a country, can exercise significant but usually limited influence on a few relevant issues in multi-religious countries. In countries with one dominant religion, especially with a state religion, relevant religious leaders and religious MAs can have much more influence, especially on issues relevant to the particular religious MA.

(p) Scientific-learned MAs have become increasingly powerful over the past few centuries as science has had a long series of successes in explaining our planet/world and the larger universe. Pinker (2018) has just sent to press a magisterial book reviewing the long-term impacts and benefits of science for society, which cumulatively support not only the massive, long-term impact of science on human society globally, but also strongly support the similar huge impact of scientific MAs. Storer (1966) pointed out that scientific MAs are important parts of the social system of science, as *integrative mechanisms* (p. 148). He wrote of such MAs at different territorial levels, national [and state/province] and also different levels of generality versus specificity of focus, from all scientists to scientists in a specific academic discipline (e.g., biology, economics) or specialty field within or across disciplines.

(q) Economic support MAs vary widely in their global impacts, depending on the subtype considered. I will discuss separately each subtype I have identified:

(i) Well-financed trade/business MAs (TBAs) [and also Major business firms, as for-profits, not MAs] tend to be powerful in affecting issues/decisions that can have a major financial impact on their central economic interests in democratic nation-states at all levels of economic development, but less so in authoritarian, let alone totalitarian, nation-states (Saitgalina et al., 2016).

(ii) Major trade/labor unions, especially in industrial nations (versus agrarian/pre-industrial or post-industrial nations; Galenson, 1994) and if well-financed and large in membership, tend to be powerful in affecting issues/decisions that can have a major financial impact on their central economic, professional, and/or occupational interests in democratic nation-states.

(iii) Farm owners' MAs can be powerful on relevant issues in agrarian/pre-industrial countries and early phase industrial nations, but usually tend to be weaker in socio-political influence than the prior MA types, especially in advanced modern and post-modern (post-industrial; service-technology dominant) societies/nation-states.

(iv) Farm workers' (non-farm-owners) MAs tend to be very weak in impact in any economic development level of societies. But there can be exceptions, as with the United Farm Workers (UFW) in the USA under Cesar Chavez in the late 20th century. Unfortunately, UFW success was temporary, and internal squabbles led to its decline (Bardacke, 2012).

HISTORICAL IMPACTS OF VOLUNTARY ASSOCIATIONS 77

(r) Social innovation and sustainable development MAs, active in many developing or transitional nations/societies, strive to increase or expand the socioeconomic development process. Unfortunately, in many cases their top-down, non-participative decision-making and leadership often leads to little positive impact on average. In the rather rare instances of MAs that intentionally involve local leaders/people as decision-making and practical planning participants, more positive impacts on sustainable development can be achieved.

(s) Among other major MA subtypes mentioned in my comprehensive typology of goal/purpose types above (Section E, #14), the most impact/influence on society (but rarely on the political or business system) is usually observed for Philanthropic/Charity-Social Service-Health/Medical-Education MAs and also for Community Improvement-Protection-Economic Development-Poverty Alleviation MAs, especially in developing nation-states. Self-Help-Support-Improvement-personal growth MAs often have positive impacts on their members/participants, but very rarely on the larger society. For other MA types, mainly with expressive rather than instrumental goals and activities, there are often individual/participant impacts, but few cumulative impacts on the larger society or its institutions.

(t) Some readers may wonder why I have not said much, if anything, here about *how* MAs achieve their impacts—the internal workings and operations of MAs. Other critics will point to my apparent neglect of their favorite topics, like social capital, social networks, social influence, social exchange, and such. My answer to both kinds of criticisms is that I sought here to focus centrally on longer term societal and global historical impacts of MAs as a key type of NPO. Various other documents by the author (e.g., Smith, 2000; Smith Stebbins, & Grotz, 2016) and by many others deal extensively with such matters (e.g., Block, 2004; Cnaan & Milofsky, 2008; Connors, 2001, 2012; Powell & Steimberg, 2006; Renz & Herman, 2016; Saul, 2004).

3   *Basic Thesis of This Paper*

The fundamental thesis of this paper has been that Membership Associations/ MAs/NMAs have had for the past two centuries and continue to have far more global importance, influence, and enduring impact in contemporary societies than is commonly recognized, even by most voluntaristics scholars (Smith, 2013, 2016a). A variety of kinds of supporting empirical evidence has been adduced to make this point clear and quite plausible, though there will doubtless be skeptics. Such skepticism is to be expected, given the nature of scientific revolutions and paradigm shifts, which tend to be resisted by the current top scientists in any field or discipline, protecting their long-term career interests (Kuhn, 1962). The collective wisdom and dominant theoretical paradigm of voluntaristics scholars/researchers worldwide at present argues to the contrary of my main thesis, viewing nonprofit agencies/Volags/NPAs as the most important, consequential, and high-global-impact aspect of the VNPS, both now and in the past (especially the past two centuries or so).

The author contends that the foregoing conventional wisdom/dominant paradigm of the emergent voluntaristics academic discipline (Smith, 2016a) is misguided and just plain wrong. Too many scholars in the field mistake Volag/NPA paid staff numbers and the wealth/income in nonprofit agencies for long-term/historical power and impact/influence, failing to "see the forest for the trees." Also, the dominant paradigm seems misguided and far too *status quo*-oriented in believing that routine services, however valuable cumulatively, as provided by Volags/NPAs are more important than the fundamental and systemic, societal and historical, often global, sociocultural changes and often ethical evolution caused by the 13 types of significant impact MAs as reviewed here. Far too many voluntaristics scholars/academics fail to understand the deep truth in INDEPENDENT SECTOR Founding President, Brian O'Connell's, widely quoted statement that advocacy is "the quintessential function of the voluntary sector" (O'Neill, 1989, p. 114).

De Wit et al. recently (2017) made this same point with a focus on volunteering, rather than on NPOs, but the two versions are opposite but integrally connected sides of the same coin: production of services is *much* less important in the societal or larger global context long term than social innovation, usually involving advocacy, in which many MA types specialize, but very few Volags/NPAs do.

Rochester (2013; see also the Introduction by Rochester to present issue, Vol. 2, Nos. 5–6, of this journal, *Voluntaristics Review*) has the right idea, and presents quite well his version of the case for voluntary action and the impact of MAs, where most voluntary action and volunteering take place (Smith, 2014c). Smith (2000, pp. 217–241; Chap. 10) argues that those scholars who overemphasize nonprofit agencies as NPOs to the virtual neglect of MAs are not only misguided and myopic, but commit the fallacies of following various flat-earth paradigms about the VNPS:

> The *Paid-Staff Voluntary Group Flat-Earth Paradigm* (pp. 222–224).
> The *Traditional-Nonmember-Service Flat-Earth Paradigm* (pp. 227–228).
> The *Money-Is-the-Key Flat-Earth Paradigm* (p. 232).
> The *Formalized Group Flat-Earth Paradigm* (pp. 234–235).

HISTORICAL IMPACTS OF VOLUNTARY ASSOCIATIONS 79

4   *Smith's Prior Round-Earth Map/Approach for VNPS Study (Smith, 2000, pp. 217–242, Chap. 10)*

Developing and using a round-earth paradigm, as sketched in Smith (2000, pp. 217–242), to understand the VNPS and to pursue voluntaristics research properly is highly recommended. This suggestion applies to understanding MA impact/influence as well as to any other topical aspect of voluntaristics (Smith, 2016a). Quoted here with permission, Smith's Round-Earth Paradigm sketch for voluntaristics research (2000, pp. 238–240) is as follows:

(1)   Viewing the VNPS [nonprofit or third sector; civil society; solidary-social economy] as important for social science scholarship, VNPS practice, and the whole of society or any other sociopolitical territorial unit.

(2)   Viewing the business, government, and nonprofit/voluntary sectors (including GAS) of a nation or other sociopolitical territories as three of the important sectors of society, but also including the household or family sector broadly interpreted as a fourth sector that probably arose first in human history as groups.

(3)   Viewing work organizations, including paid-staff VGS, as one important kind of organization, one aspect of society, and one focus of social science scholarship, but also including volunteer and membership groups, like GAS [and other MAS], and their volunteers at any territorial level of scope in one's round-earth VNPS paradigm.

(4)   Including social movement/protest GAS and activities as important to the VNPS and worthy of study, because of their importance in actually changing human society in a long-term way (for instance, see Gamson, 1990). But also including the much larger set of groups and volunteers who are *not* working on sociopolitical change, let alone using protest at all, as well as a minority of the latter using protest to maintain the status quo or to reverse changes already made by social movements and protest.

(5)   Including modern, member benefit, mutual aid, self-help, and advocacy GAS [plus other MAS] and activities in the VNPS paradigm, as well as the more traditional, personal social service GAS [and other MAS] which attempt to help nonmembers, often mistakenly calling themselves 'public benefit' groups as if only they were VGS [MAS] with benefits for the public. In the aggregate, both member benefit and nonmember benefit GAS serve the public.

(6)   Including in the round earth view the large majority of mainstream, non-deviant ('angelic') GAS [and other MAS] as well as the more

deviant ('damned') and potentially or actually stigmatized deviant GAS [and other MAS]. The deviant GAS may exhibit only minor and temporary deviance by a minority of their members, or may manifest a more fundamental deviance throughout the GA, often from its initial formation.

(7) Understanding that money is *not* the key to understanding GAS [and other MAS], because their principal resource is the commitment of their members and its manifestation in the volunteer activities of such members. The small amount of money needed by a GA can usually be raised easily by charging dues or getting donations from members, along with some modest fund-raising events to which nonmembers are invited. Meeting space is usually obtained at no or low cost.

(8) Realizing that GAS have been found all over the world for many millennia. They also have been found, when sought by appropriate methodology (Appendix 1), in all or nearly all existing nations and territories inhabited by humans since at least 10,000 years ago. Nonetheless, there may be socioculturally unique factors at any territorial level of scope in any nation that explain in part the nature of the VNPS there, including GAS [and other MAS].

(9) Using a variety of analytical type classifications (see Smith, 1996, 1995d; Smith et al., 1973; [Smith, Stebbins, & Grotz, 2016: Chapter 3]) for VGS [MAS] as well as one or more purposive type classifications, preferably a revised ICNPO (Salamon & Anheier, 1992; Smith, 1996) rather than the cumbersome NTEE (Hodgkinson & Toppe, 1991).

(10) Doing some historical study of the phenomena of interest in order to understand something of the context out of which current phenomena have grown. In the same vein, historians might spend more time relating their work to current phenomena to the extent possible.

(11) Integrating study of developing country phenomena with developed country VNPS phenomena, seeking both similarities and differences.

(12) Studying semi-formal and even informal GAS as well as formalized GAS and paid-staff VGS [MAS].

(13) Integrating churches and other religious VGS and their volunteers into the study of GAS [and other MAS] and other VNPS phenomena.

(14) Going beyond sociodemographic predictors in studying individual volunteer participation, including such factors as personality traits, attitudes, intelligence, situational characteristics, and environment.

HISTORICAL IMPACTS OF VOLUNTARY ASSOCIATIONS 81

(15) Studying the entire inter-organizational field or population of organizations in which given VGS are embedded, in addition to analyzing the internal structure and processes of plus resource attraction by individual VGS.

(16) Being open to the potential existence of additional Flat-Earth Paradigms that I have ignored here, which will require suitable further attention in a still-better Round-Earth VNPS Paradigm than I have sketched above and the list of Flat-Earth Paradigms presented in this Chapter."

G   Recent Trends and Research Needed

The global impacts of the VNPS, and especially of associations/MAS/NMAS, have been growing throughout recent history, especially since the Industrial Revolution and its accompanying Organizational Revolution, beginning c. 1800 CE in various nations. Overviews of the recent history of social movements and of specific social movement organizations (SMOS; Lofland, 1996), which are nearly always political voluntary associations, make this clear qualitatively (Tilly, 2004). Careful, systematic research on SMOS examined over decades and centuries, such as that by Gamson (1990), provides quantitative evidence of the powerful, often global, impacts of certain membership associations (MAS) and types of MAS, particularly SMOS. Gamson (1990, p. 52), for instance, showed that about half of his random sample of SMOS (*challenging groups*, in his terminology) in the USA from 1800–1945, usually national MAS or involving such MAS (e.g., Smith, Pospisilova, & Wu, 2016) achieved significant new advantages—changes in the national, sociocultural system that they sought. Other research on SMS/SMOS cited above corroborates most of Gamson's conclusions.

Thus, the most pressing need for future research on MA impacts is for large-scale, systematic, comparative studies of the 13 kinds of MAS reviewed in this paper, perhaps only using published, secondary materials. We have seen here two exemplary models for how best to do such research (1) Gamson's (1990) book reporting on 145 years of SMO outcomes in the USA and their probable, causal antecedents for a random sample of national SMOS, comprised of MAS: and (2) Burstein and Linton's (2002) article reviewing the degree and types of influence of SMS/SMOS, political parties, and political interest groups in the prior decade of published research in selected journals, along with the presence of relevant causal antecedents of the outcomes. By combining these two related methodologies for a broad sample of nations and world regions, and also expanding the range of MA types studied to include all of the 13 types discussed in the present article, one can expect to provide better, more general conclusions about MA impact in the recent history of the world.

H Usable Knowledge

1 *Summary of the Research Reviewed*
The simplest summary of the research reviewed here is that *voluntary associations/MAS/NMAS, and the volunteers who form the backbone of their activities and achievements, have contributed positively and significantly, at times substantially, to socio-cultural progress, human satisfaction/happiness, and ethical evolution for a vast range of human goals and valuable outcomes, especially since about 1800 and the Industrial and Organizational Revolutions. This process has occurred especially in democratic nations or societies with effective civil liberties, but also in authoritarian or even totalitarian nations at times.* However, MAS and their dedicated, if sometimes misguided or simply harmful, leaders and volunteers, have also at times fostered very negative outcomes for their societies, as Smith (2018b) shows. There is virtually no imaginable outcome, positive or negative, societally beneficial or harmful, that MAS and their formal volunteers could not foster, even achieve, if enough people grasped the vision and dedicated their hearts, time, and treasure long-term to its accomplishment. By contrast, nothing could be further from the truth regarding volunteer service programs (VSPS) in larger parent organizations and their very limited impact potentials (Rochester, 2013; see also Brudney et al., 2016).

This limited impact conclusion is also true for Volags/nonprofit agencies/NPAS, whose services mainly have had less substantial, more routine, status-quo-oriented, historical impacts on a society/nation or on the emerging global human society. *Failure to understand these facts about MAS/NMAS versus Volags/nonprofit agencies/NPAS seriously biases most research on the total impact of NPOS and the VNPS, where myopia and a too-narrow focus seem to blind scholars/academics to the larger view of the "forest," not just the individual "trees."* It is to be hoped that this paper will open some academics' eyes to the crucial larger global and historical context of MA impact. Part of the problem lies in the failure of many academics to consider and identify as MAS the full range of 13 relevant types of NPGS/NPOS reviewed here.

2 *The Need for a Paradigm Shift in Voluntaristics/Nonprofits Research Regarding MAS/NMAS*
Based on the extensive research on MAS reviewed in this paper, I argue that a solid case can be made for voluntaristics scholars/academics to undergo a

HISTORICAL IMPACTS OF VOLUNTARY ASSOCIATIONS 83

paradigm shift (Kuhn, 1962) in their thinking about the relative importance of MAS/NMAS as contrasted with Volags/nonprofit agencies/NPAS and other key NPO types (Smith, 2017a, 2017c). Such a shift is consistent with new ways of producing knowledge, and themes such as trans-disciplinarity, complexity-heterogeneity, and reflexivity (Gibbons et al., 1994).

All types of MAS need to be studied more carefully and fully whenever NPOS or the whole VNPS are the focus, rather than often being ignored as invisible or inconsequential *dark matter* (Smith, 1997a, 1997c). Most people, including voluntaristics scholars/academics, are misled by thinking about MAS in far too narrow terms, as Scouts, Alcoholics Anonymous/AA, school or university clubs, or sports associations. The correct definition of an MA as an NPO fits the 13 more important types of MAS reviewed here that have brought about significant, sometimes substantial, and often enduring positive changes in specific societies as ethical evolution and various rights revolutions, especially in nation-states since about 1800, and in the global human society as a whole during this period.

I   Bibliography

Abanes, Richard. (1996). *American militias: Rebellion, racism & religion.* Downers Grove, IL: Intervarsity Press.

Abbott, A. (1988). *The system of professions.* Chicago, IL: University of Chicago Press.

Abdalla, A. (2008). *The student movement and national politics in Egypt: 1923–1973.* Cairo: American University of Cairo Press.

Aboul-Einein, Y. H. (2013). *Militant Islamist ideology.* Annapolis, MD: Naval Institute Press.

Adam, B. A. (1995). *The rise of a gay and lesbian movement,* rev. ed., New York: Twayne.

Adams, Tyrone L. & Smith, Stephen A. (2008). *Electronic tribes: The virtual worlds of geeks, gamers, shamans, and scammers.* Austin, TX: University of Texas Press.

Adkins, R. E. (2008). *The evolution of political parties, campaigns, and elections: Landmark documents, 1787–2007.* Washington, DC: CQ Press.

Ahmed, S. & Potter, D. (2006). *NGOs in international politics.* West Hartford, CT: Kumarian Press.

Aldrich, J. H. (1995). *Why parties? The origin and transformation of political parties in America.* Chicago, IL: University of Chicago Press.

Aldrich, J. H. (2011). *Why parties? A second look.* Chicago, IL: University of Chicago Press.

Allen, W. S. (1984). *The Nazi seizure of power.* New York: Franklin Watt.

Amenta, E. (1998). *When movements matter: The Townsend plan and the rise of social security.* Princeton, NJ: Princeton University Press.

Amenta, E, Caren, N., Chiarello, E., & Su, Y. (2010). The political consequences of social movements. *Annual Review of Sociology, 36*, 287–307.

American Sociological Association. (2013). Altruism, morality, and social solidarity. Section introduction, www.asanet.org/sections/altruism.cfm. Accessed December 15, 2017.

Anderson, G. L., and Herr, K. G. (2007). *Encyclopedia of activism and social justice.* (3 vols.). Thousand Oaks, CA: SAGE.

Anderson, R. T. (1973). Voluntary associations in history: From Paleolithic to present times. In D. H. Smith (Ed.), *Voluntary action research: 1973* (pp. 9–28). Lexington, MA: Lexington Books.

Andrews, K. T. (1997). The impacts of social movements on the political process: The civil rights movement and black electoral politics in Mississippi. *American Sociological Review, 62*(5), 800–819.

Andrews, K. T. & Edwards, B. (2004). Advocacy organizations in the U.S. political process. *Annual Review of Sociology, 30*, 479–506.

Andrews, K. T., Ganz, M., Baggetta, M., Han, H., & Chaeyoon Lim. (2010). Leadership, membership, and voice: Civic associations that work. *American Journal of Sociology, 115*(4), 1191–1242.

Anheier, H. K. (1987). Indigenous voluntary associations, nonprofits, and development in Africa. In W. W. Powell (Ed.), *The nonprofit sector* (pp. 416–433). New Haven, CT: Yale University Press.

Anheier, H. K. (2004). *Civil society: Measurement, evaluation, policy.* London: Earthscan.

Aptheker, H. (1989). *Abolitionism: A revolutionary movement.* Boston, MA: Twayne.

Armstrong, K. (2000). *Holy war: The Crusades and their impact on today's world.* New York: Anchor Books.

Armstrong, K. (2001). *The battle for God: Fundamentalism in Judaism, Christianity, and Islam.* New York: Harper Collins Publishers Ltd.

Armstrong, K. (2004). *A history of God: The 4,000-year quest of Judaism, Christianity, and Islam.* New York: Gramercy Books, Random House.

Armstrong, K. (2014). *Fields of blood: Religion and the history of violence.* New York: Knopf.

Assael, H. (1968). The political role of trade associations in distributive conflict resolution. *Journal of Marketing, 32*, 21–28.

Atlas, J. (2010). *Seeds of change: The story of ACORN, America's most controversial antiproverty community organizing group.* Nashville, TN: Vanderbilt University Press.

Aubrac, L. (1993). *Outwitting the Gestapo.* Lincoln, NE: University of Nebraska Press.

Avalos, H. (2005). *Fighting words: The origins of religious violence.* Amherst, NY: Prometheus Books.

Ayoob, M. (2007). *The many faces of political Islam.* Ann Arbor, MI: University of Michigan Press.

Azaransky, S. (Ed.). (2013). *Religion and politics in America's borderlands.* Lexington, MA: Lexington Books.

Backhouse, R. E. & Fontaine, P. (Eds.). (2010). *The history of the social sciences since 1945.* Cambridge: Cambridge University Press.

Baggett, J. P. (2001). *Habitat for humanity: Building private homes, building public religion.* Philadelphia, PA: Temple University Press.

Bakal, C. (1979). *Charity USA.* New York: Times Books.

Banaszak, L. A. (1996). *Why movements succeed or fail: Opportunity, culture, and the struggle for woman suffrage.* Princeton, NJ: Princeton University Press.

Barber, B. R. (1984). *Strong democracy: Participatory politics for a new age.* Berkeley, CA: University of California Press.

Bardacke, Frank. (2012). *Trampling out the vintage: Cesar Chavez and the two souls of the United Farm Workers.* Brooklyn, NY: Verso.

Barnett, J. (2001). *The meaning of environmental security: Ecological politics and policy in the new security era.* London: Zed Books.

Bassett, T. J. (2003). Dangerous pursuits: Hunter associations (Donzo Ton) and national politics in Côte D'Ivoire. *Africa, 73*(1), 1–30.

Batinic, J. (2015). *Women and Yugoslav partisans: A history of World War II resistance.* Cambridge: Cambridge University Press.

Baumgartner, F. R., Berry, J. M., Hojnacki, M., Kimball, D. C., & Leech, Beth L. (2009). *Lobbying and policy change: Who wins, who loses, and why.* Chicago, IL: University of Chicago Press.

Baumgartner, F. R. & Leech B. L. (1998). *Basic interests: The importance of groups in politics and in political science.* Princeton, NJ: Princeton University Press.

Baumgartner, F. R. & Leech, B. L. (2001). Interest niches and policy bandwagons: Patterns of interest group involvement in national politics. *Journal of Politics, 63*(4), 1191–1213.

Bebbington, A., Hickey, S., & Mitlin, D. C. (Eds.) (2008). *Can NGOs make a difference? The challenge of development alternatives.* London: Zed Books.

Becker, D. G. (1990). Business associations in Latin America: The Venezuelan case. *Comparative Political Studies, 23*(1), 114–138.

Beito, D. T. (2000). *From mutual aid to the welfare state: Fraternal Societies and Social services, 1890–1967.* Chapel Hill, NC: The University of North Carolina Press.

Bell, S. & Morse, S. (2008). *Sustainable indicators: Measuring the immeasurable?* 2nd edn. London: Routledge.

Bellah, R. N. (2011). *Religion in human evolution: From the Paleolithic to the axial age.* Cambridge, MA: Harvard University Press.

Bennett, M. R. (2015). Religiosity and formal volunteering in global perspective. In J. Haers, J. Von Essen, L. Hustinx, & S. Mels (Eds.), *Religion and volunteering* (pp. 77–96). New York: Springer International Publishing.

Bennett, R. J. (1997). The impact of European economic integration on business associations: The UK case. *West European Politics, 20*(3), 61–90.

Berger, P. L. (1999). *The desecularization of the world: Resurgent religion and world politics.* Grand Rapids, MI: Wm. B. Eerdmans.

Berman, S. (1997). Civil society and the collapse of the Weimar republic. *World Politics, 49*(03), 401–429.

Bernal, V. (2014). *Theorizing NGOs: States, feminisms, and neoliberalism.* Durham, NC: Duke University Press Books.

Berry, J. M. (1997). *The interest group society.* 3rd edn. New York: Addison-Wesley Longman.

Berry, J. M., with D. F. Arons. (2005). *A voice for nonprofits.* Washington, DC: The Brookings Institution.

Berry, J. M. & Wilcox, C. (2008). *The interest group society*, 5th edn. Upper Saddle River, NJ: Pearson.

Berry, J. M., Portney, K. E., & Thomson, K. (1993). *The rebirth of urban democracy.* Washington, DC: The Brookings Institution.

Beyers, J. (2002). Gaining and seeking access: The European adaptation of domestic interest associations. *European Journal of Political Research, 41*(5), 585–612.

Beyers, J., Eising, R., & Maloney, W. (2008). Researching interest group politics in Europe and elsewhere: Much we study, little we know? *Western European Politics, 31*(6), 1103–1128.

Blackburn, R. (2011). *The overthrow of colonial slavery: 1776–1848.* London: Verso.

Blair, K. J. (1994). *The torchbearers: Women & their amateur arts associations in America, 1890–1930.* Bloomington, IN: Indiana University Press.

Blakeley, R. (2007). Bringing the state back into terrorism studies. *European Political Science, 6*(3), 228–235.

Blanchard, D. A. (1994). *The anti-anti-abortion movement and the rise of the religious right.* New York: Twayne.

Block, S. R. (2004). *Why nonprofits fail.* San Francisco, CA: Jossey-Bass.

Blumberg, R. L. (1991). *Civil rights: The 1960s freedom struggle*, rev. edn. New York: Twayne Publishers.

Bob, C. (2012). *The global right wing and the clash of world politics.* Cambridge: Cambridge University Press.

Bobbio, N. (1989). *Democracy and dictatorship: The nature and limits of state power.* Minneapolis: University of Minnesota Press.

Boix, C. (1998). *Political parties, growth and equality: Conservative and social democratic economic strategies in the world economy.* Cambridge: Cambridge University Press.

Boli, J. & Thomas, G. M. (Eds.) (1999). *Constructing world culture: International nongovernmental organizations since 1875.* Stanford, CA: Stanford University Press.

Bonnett, C. E. (1956). *History of employers' associations in the United States*. New York: Vantage Press.

Borkman, T. J. (1999). *Understanding self-help/mutual aid*. New Brunswick, NJ: Rutgers University Press.

Borras Jr, Saturnino M., Edelman, M., & Kay, C. (2008). Transnational agrarian movements: Origins and politics, campaigns and impact. *Journal of Agrarian Change, 8*(2–3), 169–204.

Boulding, K. (1953). *The organizational revolution*. New York: Harper.

Bradfield, R. M. (1973). *A natural history of associations*. 2 vols. London: Duckworth.

Bresler, R. J. (2004). *Freedom of association: Rights and liberties under the law*. Santa Barbara, CA: ABC-CLIO.

Bresler, R. J., et al. (2016). Civil liberties and freedoms as association contexts. In D. H. Smith, R. A. Stebbins, & J. Grotz (Eds.), *Palgrave handbook of volunteering, civic participation, and nonprofit associations* (Chapter 45, pp. 1093–1115). Basingstoke: Palgrave Macmillan.

Breuilly, J. (2013). *The Oxford handbook of the history of nationalism*. Oxford: Oxford University Press.

British Medical Association. (1986). *Smoking out the barons: The campaign against the tobacco industry*. New York: Wiley.

Brooks, A. C. (2008). *Gross national happiness*. New York: Basic Books.

Broom, D. M. (2004). *The evolution of morality and religion*. New York: Cambridge University Press.

Brovkin, V. N. (1994). *Behind the front lines of the civil war: Political parties and social movements in Russia, 1918–1922*. Princeton, NJ: Princeton Legacy Press.

Brown, D. E. (1991). *Human Universals*. Boston, MA: McGraw Hill.

Brown, L. D., Shepherd, M. D., Wituk, S. A., & Meissen, G. (2007). Goal achievement and the accountability of consumer-run organizations. *The Journal of Behavioral Health Services & Research, 34*(1), 73–82.

Brudney, J. L., Lee, Y-j, Bin Afif, S. A., Ockenden, N., & Sillah, A. (2016). Formal volunteer service programs. In D. H. Smith, R. A. Stebbins, & J. Grotz (Eds.), *Palgrave handbook of volunteering, civic participation, and nonprofit associations* (pp. 330–348, Chapter 15). Basingstoke: Palgrave Macmillan.

Bruns, R. A. (2011). *Cesar Chavez and the United Farm Workers movement*. Santa Barbara, CA: ABC-CLIO.

Bucchi, M. (2004). *Science in society: An introduction to social studies of science*. Oxford: Routledge.

Bullivant, S. & Ruse, M. (2016). *The Oxford handbook of atheism*. Oxford: Oxford University Press.

Burleigh, M. (2007). *Earthly powers: The clash of religion and politics in Europe, from the French Revolution to the Great War*. New York: Harper Perennial.

Burlingame, D. F. (Ed.) (2004). *Philanthropy in America: A comprehensive historical encyclopedia*, 3 vols. Santa Barbara, CA: ABC-CLIO.

Burstein, P. & Linton, A. (2002). The impact of political parties, interest groups, and social movement organizations on public policy: Some recent evidence and theoretical concerns. *Social Forces, 81*(2), 380–408.

Butcher, J. (Ed.) (2012). *Mexican solidarity: Citizen participation and volunteering.* New York: Springer.

Bystydzienski, J. M. & Sekhon, J. (Eds.) (1999). *Democratization and women's grassroots movement.* Bloomington, IN: Indiana University Press.

Cable, S. & Degutis, B. (1997). Movement outcomes and dimensions of social change: The multiple effects of local mobilizations. *Current Sociology/Sociologie Contemporaine, 45,* 121–135.

Calhoun, G. M. (1970). *Athenian clubs in politics and litigation.* Austin, TX: University of Texas Press.

Cameron, K. S. (1982). *Organizational effectiveness: A comprehensive bibliography.* Boulder, CO: National Center for Higher Education Management Systems.

Campbell, C. M. (1962). *The Farm Bureau and the New Deal: A study of the making of national farm policy, 1933–40.* Urbana, IL: University of Illinois Press.

Carmichael, C. (2002). *Ethnic cleansing in the Balkans.* London: Routledge.

Carmin, J. (1999). Voluntary Associations, professional organisations and the environmental movement in the United States. *Environmental Politics, 8*(1), 101–121.

Carsten, F. L. (1982). *War against war: British and German radical movements in the First World War.* Berkeley, CA: University of California Press.

Carter, R. (1961). *The gentle legions.* Garden City, NY: Doubleday.

Casey, J. (2015). *The nonprofit world: Civil society and the rise of the nonprofit sector.* Boulder, CO: Lynne Rienner.

Cash, A. (2003). *Deep inside the underground economy.* Berlin: Breakout Productions.

Castles, F. G. (1982). *The impact of parties: politics and policies in democratic capitalist states.* London & Beverly Hills, CA: Sage Publications.

Castro, D. (1999). *Revolution and revolutionaries: Guerrilla movements in Latin America.* Wilmington, DE: SR Books.

Cattell, J. M. (2016 [1904]). *Scientific societies and associations.* London: Forgotten Books.

Chalk, Peter (Ed.). (2012). *Encyclopedia of terrorism.* Santa Barbara, CA: ABC-CLIO.

Chamberlain, J., McDonagh, R., Lalonde, A., & Arulkumaran, S. (2003). The role of professional associations in reducing maternal mortality worldwide. *International Journal of Gynecology & Obstetrics, 83*(1), 94–102.

Chambers, C. A. (1985). The historical role of the voluntary sector in human service delivery in urban America. In G. Tobin (Ed.), *Social planning and human service delivery in the voluntary sector* (pp. 3–28). Westport, CT: Greenwood Press.

Chambers, R. (1995). Rural appraisal: Rapid, relaxed and participatory. In A. Mukherjee (Ed.), *Participatory rural appraisal: Methods and applications in rural planning* (pp. 1–63, Chapter 1). New Delhi: Vikas Publishing House.

Chandra, G. (2010). Participatory rural appraisal. *Issues and Tools for Social Science Research in Inland Fisheries. Central Inland Fisheries Research Institute. Bulletin, 163*, 286–302.

Chandra, K. (Ed.) (2017). *Democratic dynasties: State, party and family in contemporary Indian politics.* Cambridge, UK: Cambridge University Press.

Charles, J. A. (1993). *Service clubs in American society: Rotary, Kiwanis, and Lions.* Urbana, IL: University of Illinois Press.

Chatfield, C. & Kleidman, R. (1992). *The American peace movement.* New York: Twayne.

Chaves, M. (2012). Religious congregations. In Lester M. Salamon (Ed.), *The State of nonprofit America*, 2nd edn (pp. 362–393). Washington, DC: Brookings Institution Press.

Christenson, L. (1994). *Skinhead street gangs.* Boulder, CO: Paladin Press.

Chroust, A.-H. (1967). Plato's academy: The first organized school of political science in antiquity. *The Review of Politics, 29*(1), 25–40.

Cigler, A. J. & Loomis, B. A. (2002). *Interest group politics*, 6th edn. Washington, DC: CQ Press.

Cigler, A. J., Loomis, B. A., & Nownes, A. J. (2015). *Interest group politics*, 9th edn. Washington, DC: CQ Press.

Clark, J. (1991). *Democratizing development: The role of voluntary organizations.* West Hartford, CT: Kumarian Press.

Clarke, P. B. (2006). *New religions in global perspective.* New York: Routledge.

Clawson, D., Neustadtl, A., & Scott, D. (1992). *Money talks: Corporate PACs and political influence.* New York: Basic Books.

Cleary, E. L. & Stewart-Gambino, H. (1996). *Power, politics, and Pentecostals in Latin America.* Boulder, CO: Westview Press.

Clemens, E. S. (1997). *The people's lobby: Organizational innovation and the rise of interest group politics in the United States, 1890–1925.* Chicago, IL: The University of Chicago Press.

Clemens, E. S. & Guthrie, D. (Eds.) (2010). *Politics and partnerships: The role of voluntary associations in America's political past and present.* Chicago, IL: The University of Chicago Press.

Clotfelter, C. T. (Ed.) (1992). *Who benefits from the nonprofit sector?* Chicago, IL: University of Chicago Press.

Cnaan, R. A. & Boddie, S. C. (2002). *The invisible caring hand: American congregations and the provision of welfare.* New York: New York University Press.

Cnaan, R. A. & Curtis, D. W. (2013). Religious congregations as voluntary associations. *Nonprofit and Voluntary Sector Quarterly, 42*(1), 7–33.

Cnaan, R. A. & Milofsky, C. (2008). *Handbook of community movements and local organizations.* New York: Springer.

Cnaan, R. A., Wineberg, R., & Boddie, S. C. (1999). *The newer deal: Social work and religion in partnership.* New York: Columbia University Press.

Cnaan, R. A., Zrinščak, S., Grönlund, H., Smith, D. H., Hu, M., Kinoti, M. D., Knorre, B., Kumar, P., & Pessi, A. B. (2016). Volunteering in religious congregations and faith-based associations. In D. H. Smith, R. A. Stebbins, & J. Grotz (Eds.), *Palgrave handbook of volunteering, civic participation, and nonprofit associations* (pp. 472–494, Chapter 22). Basingstoke: Palgrave Macmillan.

Cohen, G. (2003). Party over policy: The dominating impact of group influence on political beliefs. *Journal of Personality and Social Psychology, 85*(5), 808–822.

Colby, A. & Damon, W. (1992). *Some do care: Contemporary lives of moral commitment.* New York: Free Press.

Colburn, F. D. (1994). *The vogue of revolution in poor countries.* Princeton, NJ: Princeton University Press.

Cole, M. & Deighan, H. (2012). *Political parties in Britain.* Edinburgh: Edinburgh University Press.

Coleman, W. & Grant, W. (1988). The organizational cohesion and political access of business: A study of comprehensive associations. *European Journal of Political Research, 16*(5), 457–487.

Comaroff, J. & Stearn, P. (Eds.) (1995). *Perspectives on nationalism and war.* New York: Routledge.

Combs, C. C. & Slann, M. W. (2007). *Encyclopedia of terrorism*, rev. edn. New York: Facts on File.

Commission on Private Philanthropy and Public Needs. (1975). *Giving in America: Toward a stronger voluntary sector.* Washington, DC: CPPPN.

Comrey, A. L., Pfiffner, J. M., & High, H. P. (1952). Factors influencing organizational effectiveness. *Personnel Psychology, 5*(4), 307–328.

Connors, T. D. (2012). *The volunteer management handbook.* 2nd ed. New York: Wiley.

Connors, T. D. (2001). *The nonprofit handbook: Management.* 3rd edition. New York: Wiley.

Conradi, E. (1905). Learned societies and academies in early times. *Journal of Genetic Psychology, 12*, 384–427.

Coogan, T. P. (2002). *The IRA.* New York: St. Martin's Griffin.

Coppedge, M. & Reinicke, W. H. (1990). Measuring polyarchy. *Studies in Comparative International Development, 25*(1), 51–72.

Corbett, R. (1986). *Guerrilla warfare: from 1939 to the present day.* Maryknoll, NY: Orbis Books.

Covey, H. C., Menard, S., & Franzese, R. J. (1997). *Youth gangs*, 2nd edn. Springfield, IL: C.C. Thomas.

Cox, J. J. (2017). *From primitive to indigenous: The academic study of indigenous religions.* New York: Routledge.

Credit Union National Association. (2005). *The story of the credit union movement: People not profit*, rev. edn. Madison, WI: Center for Professional Development, Credit Union National Associations.

Critchlow, D. T. & Parker, C. H. (1998). *With us always: A history of private charity and public welfare.* Lanham, MD: Rowman and Littlefield.

Crummey, D. (Ed.) (1986). *Banditry, rebellion and social protest in Africa.* London: James Currey.

Cutt, J. & Murray, V. (2000). *Accountability and effectiveness evaluation in non-profit organizations.* London: Routledge.

Dahl, R. A. (1972). *Polyarchy: Participation and opposition.* New Haven, CT: Yale University Press.

Dahl, R. A. (1998). *On democracy.* New Haven, CT: Yale University Press.

Dalton, R. J. (1994). *The green rainbow: Environmental groups in Western Europe.* New Haven, CT: Yale University Press.

Dalton, R. J. (2013). *Citizen politics: Public opinion and political parties in advanced industrial democracies*, 6th edn. Thousand Oaks, CA: SAGE.

Dalton, R. J. & Wattenberg, M. P. (2002). *Parties without partisans: Political change in advanced industrial democracies.* New York: Oxford University Press.

Dalton, R. J. & Klingemann, H.-D. (Eds.) (2009). *The Oxford handbook of political behavior.* New York: Oxford University Press.

Darwin, C., & Wilson, E. O. (Eds.). (2005). *From so simple a beginning: Darwin's four great books.* New York: W. W. Norton.

Davidson, O. G. (1993). *Under fire: The NRA and the battle for gun control.* New York: Henry Holt.

Davies, T. (2013). *NGOs: A new history of transnational civil society.* London: C. Hurst & Co.

Davies, T., Schmitz, H. P., Appe, S., Barragan-Teran, D., Owinga, B., Raggo, P. G., & Xie, L. (2016). Transnational associations and INGOs: Macro-associations. In D. H. Smith, R. A. Stebbins, & J. Grotz (Eds.), *Palgrave handbook of volunteering, civic participation, and nonprofit associations* (pp. 836–873, Chapter 33). Basingstoke: Palgrave Macmillan.

De Knop, P., Wylleman, P., Theeboom, M., De Martelaer, K., Van Puymbroeck, L. & Wittcock, H. (1994). *Youth-friendly sports clubs: Developing an effective youth sport policy.* Brussels: VUB Press.

Dees, M. (1997). Gathering storm: America's militia threat. New York: HarperPerennial.

Della Porta, D. (2006). *Social movements, political violence, and the state: A comparative analysis of Italy and Germany.* Cambridge, UK: Cambridge University Press.

Demerath, N. J., Hall, P. D., Schmitt, T., & Williams, R. H. (Eds.). (1998). *Sacred companies: Organizational aspects of religion and religious aspects of organizations.* New York: Oxford University Press.

Depkat, V. & Martschukat, J. (2013). *Religion and politics in Europe in the United States.* Baltimore, MD: Woodrow Wilson Center Press, Johns Hopkins University Press.

de Ridder-Symoens, H. (Ed.). (1992). *A history of the university in Europe*, vol. 1. *Universities in the Middle Ages.* Cambridge: Cambridge University Press.

de Tocqueville, Alexis. (1976 [1845]). *Democracy in America*, 2 vols. New York: Knopf.

de Waal, Alex. (1997). *Famine crimes: Politics and the disaster relief industry in Africa.* Oxford: African Rights and the International African Institute (James Currey & Indiana University Press).

de Wit, A., Mensink, W., Einarsson, T., & Bekkers, R. (2017). Beyond service production: Volunteering for social innovation. *Nonprofit and Voluntary Sector Quarterly* (in press) DOI: 10.1 1777/0899764017734651.

Diamond, L. (1999). *Developing democracy: Toward consolidation.* Baltimore, MD: Johns Hopkins University Press.

Diamond, L. (2007). *The spirit of democracy: The struggle to build free societies throughout the world.* New York: Times Books, Holt.

Diaz, W. (2002). For whom and for what? The contributions of the nonprofit sector. In Lester M. Salamon (Ed.), *The state of nonprofit America* (pp. 517–535). Washington, DC: Brookings Institution Press.

Diehl, P. F. & Frederking, B. (Eds.) (2010). *The politics of global governance: international organizations in an interdependent world.* Boulder, CO: Lynne Rienner Publishers.

Domhoff, G. W. (1990). *The power elite and the state: How policy is made in America.* Chicago, IL: Aldine Transaction.

Domhoff, G. W. (2005). *Who rules America? Power, politics, and social change.* New York: McGraw-Hill Humanities/Social Sciences/Languages.

Donaldson, D. & Carlson-Thies, S. (2003). *A revolution of compassion: Faith-based groups as full partners in fighting America's social problems.* Grand Rapids, MI: Baker Books.

Douglas, J. (1983). *Why charity? The case for the third sector.* Newbury Park, CA: SAGE.

Drescher, S. (2009). *Abolition: A history of slavery and antislavery.* Cambridge: Cambridge University Press.

Duchesne, L. (1912). *Early history of the Christian church from its foundation to the end of the third century.* New York: Longman's, Green & Co.

Duffy, M. P. & Gillig, S. E. (Eds.) (2004). *Teen gangs: A global view.* Westport, CT: Greenwood Press.

Dunlap, R. E. & Mertig, A. G. (1992). *American environmentalism: The U.S. environmental movement, 1970–1990.* Philadelphia, PA: Taylor & Francis.

Dur, A. (2008). Measuring interest group influence in the EU: A note on methodology. *European Union Politics, 9*(4), 559–576.

Dur, A. & de Bievre, D. (2007a). Inclusion without influence? NGOs in European trade policy. *Journal of Public Policy, 27*(1), 79–101.

Dur, A. & de Bievre, D. (2007b). The question of interest group influence. *Journal of Public Policy, 27*(1), 1–12.

Dur, A. & Mateo, G. (2012). Who lobbies the European Union? National interest groups in a multilevel polity. *Journal of European Public Policy, 19*(7), 969–987.

Dutt, N. (2012). *Early history of the spread of Buddhism & the Buddhist schools.* St. Francis, KS: Dew Publishers.

Eberly, D. & Streeter, R. (2002). *The soul of civil society: Voluntary associations and the public value of moral habits.* Lanham, MD: Lexington Books.

Edwards, M. (2011). *The Oxford handbook of civil society.* New York: Oxford University Press.

Eising, R. (2007). Institutional context, organizational resources and strategic choices: Explaining interest group access in the European Union. *European Union Politics, 8*(3), 329–362.

Eisner, P. (2005). *The freedom line: The brave men and women who rescued Allied airmen from the Nazis during World War II.* New York: Harper Perennial.

Ellerbe, H. (1995). *The dark side of Christian history.* Orlando, FL: Morningstar & Lark.

Ellis, S. J. & Noyes, K. H. (1990). *By the people: A history of Americans as volunteers,* rev. edn. San Francisco, CA: Jossey-Bass.

Emerson, M. O., Mirola, W. A., & Monahan, S. C. (2010). *Religion matters: What sociology teaches us about religion in our world.* London: Pearson.

Eng, S., & Smith, D. H. (2016). Crime, misconduct, and dysfunctions in and by associations. In D. H. Smith, R. A. Stebbins, & J. Grotz (Eds.), *Palgrave handbook of volunteering, civic participation, and nonprofit associations* (pp. 1331–1359, Chapter 54). Basingstoke: Palgrave Macmillan.

Engler, M. & Engler, P. (2016). *This is an uprising: How nonviolent revolt is shaping the twenty-first century.* New York: Nations Books, Perseus Books Group.

English, R. (2004). *Armed struggle: The history of the IRA.* Oxford: Oxford University Press.

Epstein, S. A. (1991). *Wage labor and guilds in medieval Europe.* Chapel Hill, NC: University of North Carolina Press.

Epstein, S. A. & Prak, M. (Eds.) (2008). *Guilds, innovation, and the European economy, 1400–1800*. Cambridge: Cambridge University Press.

Esman, M. J. & Uphoff, N. T. (1984). *Local organizations: Intermediaries in local development*. Ithaca, NY: Cornell University Press.

Esmer, Y. & Pettersson, T. (2007). The effects of religion and religiosity on voting behavior. In R. J. Dalton & H.-D. Klingemann (Eds.), *The Oxford handbook of political behavior* (pp. 481–503). Oxford: Oxford University Press.

Esposito, J. (2003). *Unholy war: Terror in the name of Islam*. Oxford: Oxford University Press.

Estey, M. (1981). *The unions: Structure, development, management*, 3rd edn. San Diego, CA: Harcourt Brace Jovanovich.

Etzioni, A. (1964). *Modern organizations*. Englewood Cliffs, NJ: Prentice-Hall.

Etzioni, A. (1975). *A comparative analysis of complex organizations*, rev. edn. New York: The Free Press, Simon & Schuster.

Evans, D. (1996). Before the roll call: Interest group lobbying and public policy outcomes in house committees. *Political Research Quarterly, 49*(2), 287–304.

Fardon, R., Harris, O., Marchand, T. H., Shore, C., Strang, V., Wilson, R A., & Nuttall, M. (Eds.) (2012). *The SAGE handbook of social anthropology*. London: SAGE Publications.

Farndale, E. & Brewster, C. (2005). In search of legitimacy: personnel management associations worldwide. *Human Resource Management Journal, 15*(3), 33–48.

Faulkner, F. (2007). *Moral entrepreneurs and the campaign to ban landmines*, rev. edn. Amsterdam: Editions Rodopi.

Feld, W. J. & Jordan, R. S., with Hurwitz, L. (1994). *International organizations: A comparative approach*, 3rd edn. Westport, CT: Praeger.

Feldmann, D. (2016). *Social movements for good*. New York: Wiley.

Ferree, M. M. & Hess, B. B. (1995). *Controversy and coalition: The new feminist movement*, rev. edn. New York: Twayne.

Ferree, M. M. & Martin, P. Y. (Eds.) (1995). *Feminist organizations: Harvest of the new women's movement*. Philadelphia, PA: Temple University Press.

Filani, M. O. (1975). The role of national tourist associations in the preserving of the environment in Africa. *Journal of Travel Research, 13*(4), 7–12.

Finke, R. & Stark, R. (2005). *The churching of America, 1776–2005: Winners and losers in our religious economy*. New Brunswick, NJ: Rutgers University Press.

Finsen, L. & Finsen, S. (1994). *The animal rights movement in America*. New York: Twayne.

Fisher, J. (1984). Development from below: Neighborhood improvement associations in the Latin American squatter settlements. *Studies in Comparative International Development, 19*, 61–85.

Fisher, J. (1993). *The road from Rio: Sustainable development and the nongovernmental movement in the third world*. Westport, CT: Praeger.

Fisher, J. (1998). *Nongovernments: NGOs and the political development of the third world*. West Hartford, CT: Kumarian Press.

Fisher, J. (2013). *Importing democracy: The role of NGOs in South Africa, Tajikistan, & Argentina*. Dayton, OH: Kettering Foundation Press.

Fisher, R. (1994). *Let the people decide: Neighborhood organizing in America*, rev. edn. New York: Twayne Publishers.

Fishman, J. J. (2007). *The faithless fiduciary and the quest for charitable accountability 1200–2005*. Durham, NC: Carolina Academic Press.

Fite, G. G. (1981). *American farmers: The new minority*. Bloomington, IN: Indiana University Press.

Florini, A. M. (Ed.) (2000). *The third force: The rise of transnational civil society*. Washington, DC: Carnegie Endowment for International Peace.

Flynn, P. & Hodgkinson, V. A. (Eds.) (2002). *Measuring the impact of the nonprofit sector*. New York: Springer.

Forbes, D. P. 1998. Measuring the unmeasurable: Empirical studies of nonprofit organization effectiveness from 1977 to 1997. *Nonprofit and Voluntary Sector Quarterly, 27*(2), 183–202.

Ford, H. E. & Ford, J. L. (1996). *The power of association: Success through volunteerism and positive associations*. Dubuque, IA: Kendall/Hunt.

Fordham, B. O. & McKeown, T. J. (2003). Selection and influence: Interest groups and Congressional voting on trade policy. *International Organization, 57*(3), 519–549.

Fowler, R. B., Hertzke, A. D. Olson, L. R., & Den Dulk, Kevin R. (2013). *Religion and politics in America*. Boulder, CO: Westview Press.

Fox, J. A. & Brown, L. D. (Eds.) (1998). *The struggle for accountability: The World Bank, NGOs, and grassroots movements*. Cambridge, MA: MIT Press.

Freeden, M., Sargent, L. T., & Stears, M. (Eds.). (2015). *The Oxford handbook of political ideologies*. Oxford: Oxford University Press.

Frey, R. S., Dietz, T., & Kalof, L. (1992). Characteristics of successful American protest groups: Another look at Gamson's strategy of social protest. *American Journal of Sociology, 98*, 368–387.

Friedlander, S. (2008). *Nazi Germany and the Jews, 1939–1945: The years of extermination*. New York: Harper Perennial.

Friedrich, C. J. & Brzezinski, Z. K. (1956). *Totalitarian dictatorship and autocracy*. Cambridge, MA: Harvard University Press.

Fung, A. (2003). Associations and democracy: Between theories, hopes, and realities. *Annual Review of Sociology, 29*, 515–539.

Fung, A. (2006). *Empowered participation: Reinventing urban democracy*. Princeton, NJ: Princeton University Press.

Funk, A. L. (1992). *Hidden ally: The French resistance, special operations, and the landings in southern France, 1944*. Westport, CT: Greenwood Publishing Group.

Gadd, Ian A. & Wallis, P. (Eds.) (2006). *Guilds and associations in Europe, 900–1900.* London: Centre for Metropolitan History, University of London.

Galenson, W. (1994). *Trade union growth and decline.* Westport, CT: Praeger.

Gall, G., Wilkinson, A. & Hurd, R. (Eds.) (2012). *The international handbook of labour unions.* Cheltenham: Edward Elgar.

Gamm, G. & Putnam, R. D. (1999). The growth of voluntary associations in America, 1840–1940. *Journal of Interdisciplinary History, 29*(4), 511–557.

Gamson, W. (1990). *The strategy of social protest,* 2nd edn. Belmont, CA: Wadsworth Publishing Co.

Gamwell, F. I. (1984). *Beyond preference: Liberal theories of independent association.* Chicago, IL: University of Chicago Press.

Garner, R. & Jaggard, L. (2011). *Environmental politics,* 3rd edn. Basingstoke: Palgrave Macmillan.

Gartner, A. & Riessman, F. (1984). *The self-help revolution.* New York: Human Sciences Press.

George, J. & Wilcox, L. (1996). *American extremists: Militias, supremacists, klansmen, communists, & others.* Amherst, NY: Prometheus Books.

Georgopoulos, B. S. & Tannenbaum, A. S. (1957). A study of organizational effectiveness. *American Sociological Review, 22*(5), 534–540.

Gerber, E. R. (1999). *The populist paradox: Interest group influence and the promise of direct legislation.* Princeton, NJ: Princeton University Press.

Gibbons, M., Limoges, C., Nowotny, H., Schwartzman, S., Scott, P., & Trow, M. (1994). *The new production of knowledge: The dynamics of science and research in contemporary societies.* Thousand Oaks, CA: SAGE.

Gilbert, D. (1991). *Sandinistas.* New York: Wiley-Blackwell.

Gildea, R. (2015). *Fighters in the shadows: A new history of the French resistance.* Cambridge, MA: The Belknap Press, Harvard University.

Gillion, D. Q. (2013). *The political power of protest: Minority activism and shifts in public policy.* New York: Cambridge University Press.

Gittell, M. (1980). *The limits to citizen participation: The decline of community organizations.* Beverly Hills, CA: Sage.

Gittel, R. & Vidal, A. (1998). *Community organizing: Building social capital as a development strategy.* Thousand Oaks, CA: Sage.

Gitterman, A. & Shulman, L. (Eds.) (1994). *Mutual aid groups, vulnerable populations, and the life cycle.* New York: Columbia University Press.

Giugni, M. (1998). Was it worth the effort? The outcomes and consequences of social movements. *Annual Review of Sociology, 24,* 371–393.

Giugni, M. (2004). *Social protest and policy change: Ecology, antinuclear, and peace movements in comparative perspective.* Lanham, MD: Rowman & Littlefield.

Giugni, M., McAdam, D., & Tilly, C. (1999). *How social movements matter.* Minneapolis, MN: University of Minnesota Press.

Givel, M. S. & Glantz, S. A. (2001). Tobacco lobby political influence on US state legislatures in the 1990s. *Tobacco Control, 10*, 124–134.

Glaser, B. G. & Strauss, A. L. (1967). *The discovery of grounded theory: Strategies for qualitative research*. Chicago, IL: Aldine Atherton.

Gokturk, A., Bell, D., McCortney, T., & Karaman, S. (Eds.). (2017). *National trade and professional associations of the United States 2017*, 52nd edn. Bethesda, MD: AssociationExecs.com, Columbia Books.

Gold, S. D. (2010). *Americans with Disabilities Act*. Salt Lake City, UT: Benchmark Books.

Golden, M. M. (1998). Interest groups in the rule-making process: Who participates? What voices get heard? *Journal of Public Administration Research & Theory, 8*(2), 245–270.

Goldfield, M. (1989). *The decline of organized labor in the United States*. Chicago, IL: University of Chicago Press.

Goldman, L. (2007). *Science, reform, and politics in Victorian Britain: The Social Science Association 1857–1886*. New York: Cambridge University Press.

Goldsmith, A. A. (2002). Business associations and better governance in Africa. *Public Administration and Development, 22*(1), 39–49.

Goldstein, K. M. (1999). *Interest groups, lobbying, and participation in America*. Cambridge: Cambridge University Press.

Goldstone, Jack A. (1991). *Revolution and rebellion in the early modern world*. Berkeley, CA: University of California Press.

Goodman, P. S., Pennings, J. M., & Associates. (1977). *New perspectives on organizational effectiveness*. San Francisco, CA: Jossey-Bass.

Goodwin, J. (2001). *No other way out: States and revolutionary movements, 1945–1991 (Cambridge Studies in Comparative Politics)*. New York: Cambridge University Press.

Gora, J. G. & Morris Nemerowicz, G. (1985). *Emergency squad volunteers: Professionalism in unpaid work*. New York: Praeger.

Gray, P. (2016). *Varieties of religious invention: Founders and their functions in history*. Oxford: Oxford University Press.

Greeley, A. (1972). *The denominational society*. Glenview, IL: Scott, Foresman.

Green, J. C. (2010). The party faithful: Religion and party politics in America. In S. Maisel & J. M. Berry (Eds.), *The Oxford handbook of American political parties and interest groups* (pp. 142–161). Oxford: Oxford University Press.

Greenwood, J. & Ronit, K. (1994). Interest groups in the European Community: Newly emerging dynamics and forms. *West European Politics, 17*(1), 31–52.

Greenwood, R., Suddaby, R., & Hinings, C. R. (2002). Theorizing change: The role of professional associations in the transformation of institutionalized fields. *Academy of Management Journal, 45*(1), 58–80.

Gross, R. A. ([1976] 2002). *The minutemen and their world*. New York: Hill and Wang.

Gunaratna, R. (2002). *Inside Al Qaeda: Global network of terror*. New York: Columbia University Press.

Gunn, C. (2004). *Third-sector development: Making up for the market.* Ithaca, NY: ILR Press, Cornell University Press.

Gunther, R. & Diamond, L. (2003). Species of political parties: A new typology. *Party Politics, 9*(2), 167–199.

Guo, Chao, Xu, Jun, Smith, D. H. & Zhang, Zhibin. (2012). Civil society, Chinese style: The rise of the nonprofit sector in China. *Nonprofit Quarterly,* Fall, 20–27.

Guptat, D. (2009). The power of incremental outcomes: How small victories and defeats affect social movement organizations. *Mobilization, 14*(4), 417–432.

Hakonson, B. (2013). *How to succeed with nonprofit trade and professional associations.* Colorado Springs, CO: CreateSpace Independent Publishing Platform.

Hall, P. D. (1992). *Inventing the nonprofit sector and other essays on philanthropy, volunteerism, and nonprofit organizations.* Baltimore, MD: The Johns Hopkins University Press.

Hall, P. D. (2006). A historical overview of philanthropy, voluntary associations, and nonprofit organizations in the United States, 1600–2000. In W. W. Powell & R. Steinberg (Eds.), *The nonprofit sector: A research handbook,* 2nd edn (pp. 32–65). New Haven, CT: Yale University Press.

Hall, R. H. (1972). *Organizations: Structure and process.* Englewood Cliffs, NJ: Prentice-Hall.

Hall, S. (2011). *Rethinking the American anti-war movement.* New York: Routledge.

Hamm, M. S. (1994). *American Skinheads: The criminology and control of hate crime.* Westport, CT: Praeger.

Hammack, D. C. (Ed.) (1998). *Making the nonprofit sector in the United States: A reader.* Bloomington, IN: Indiana University Press.

Hammer, O. & Rothstein, M. (Eds.) (2012). *The Cambridge companion to new religious movements.* Cambridge: Cambridge University Press.

Hancock, G. (1992). *Lords of poverty: The power, prestige, and corruption of the international aid business.* New York: Atlantic Monthly Press.

Handy, F., Kassam, M., Feeney, S., & Ranade, B. (2007). *Grass-roots NGOs by women for women: The driving force of development in India.* New Delhi: Sage Publications.

Hansmann, H. B. (1980). The role of nonprofit enterprise. *Yale Law Journal, 89*(5), 835–901.

Harland, P. A. (2003). *Associations, synagogues and congregations: Claiming a place in ancient Mediterranean society.* Minneapolis, MN: Fortress Press.

Harner, M. (2012). *Developing professional skills: Business associations.* St. Paul, MN: West Academic Publishing.

Harris, B. & Bridgen, P. (Eds.) (2007). *Charity and mutual aid in Europe and North America since 1800.* New York: Routledge.

Harris, B., Morris, A., Ascough, R. S. Chikoto, G. L. Elson, P. R. McLoughlin, J. Muukkonen, M., Pospíšilová, T., Rokal, K., Smith, D. H., Soteri-Proctor, A., Tumanova, A., & Yu, P. (2016). History of associations and volunteering. In D. H. Smith, R. A. Stebbins, &

J. Grotz (Eds.), *Palgrave handbook of volunteering, civic participation, and nonprofit associations* (pp. 23–58, Chapter 1). Basingstoke: Palgrave Macmillan.

Hartson, L. D. (1911). A study of voluntary associations, educational and social, in Europe during the period from 1100 to 1700. *Journal of Genetic Psychology, 18*, 10–30.

Haskins, J. & Stifle. J. M. (1979). *The quiet revolution: The struggle for the rights of disabled Americans*. New York: T. Y. Crowell.

Hawes, J. M. (1991). *The children's rights movement*. New York: Twayne.

Hawkins, H. (1992). *Banding together: The rise of national associations in American higher education, 1887–1950*. Baltimore, MD: Johns Hopkins University Press.

Hayden, T. (2012). *Inspiring participatory democracy: Student movements from Port Huron to today*. Boulder, CO: Paradigm Publishers.

Heinrich, V. F. (Ed.) (2011). *Civicus global survey of the state of civil society* (vol. 1). *Country profiles civil society index project 2003–2006 phase*. Bloomfield, CT: Kumarian Press Inc.

Heinrich, V. F. & Floramonti, L. (Eds.) (2008). *Civicus Global survey of the state of civil society* (vol. 2) *Comparative prospectives*. Bloomfield, CT: Kumarian Press Inc.

Heinrich, V. F. (2001). The role of NGOs in strengthening the foundations of South African democracy. *Voluntas, 12*(1), 1–15.

Herb, G. H. & Kaplan, D. H. (Eds.). (2008). *Nations and nationalism: A global historical overview*. 4 vols. Goleta, CA: ABC-CLIO.

Herman, R. D. & Renz, D. O. (2008). Advancing nonprofit organizational effectiveness research and theory: Nine theses. *Nonprofit Management & Leadership, 18*(4), 399–415.

Herring, C., Bennett, M., Gills, D., & Jenkins, N. T. (Eds.) (1998). *Empowerment in Chicago: Grassroots participation in economic development and poverty alleviation*. Chicago, IL: University of Illinois at Chicago.

Hershey, M. R. (2014). *Party politics in America*, 16th edn. New York: Routledge.

Higgins, J. (1988). *The business of medicine*. London: Macmillan.

Hirsch, B. T. & Addison J. T. (1986). *The economic analysis of unions: New approaches and evidence*. London: Taylor & Francis.

Hirst, P. (1994). *Associative democracy: New forms of economic and social governance*. Amherst, MA: University of Massachusetts Press.

Hobsbawm, E. J. 1965. *Primitive rebels: Studies in archaic forms of social movement in the 19th and 20th centuries*. New York: W. W. Norton.

Hodgkinson, V. A., & Toppe, C. (1991). A new research and planning tool for managers: The National Taxonomy of Exempt Entities. *Nonprofit Management & Leadership, 1*, 403–414.

Hodgkinson, V. A., Weitzman, M. S., & Kirsch, A. D. (1988). *From belief to commitment: The activities and finances of religious congregations in the United States*. Washington, DC: INDEPENDENT SECTOR.

Hojnacki, M., Kimball, D. C., Baumgartner, F. R., Berry, J. M., & Leech, B. L. (2012). Studying organizational advocacy and influence: Reexamining interest group research. *Annual Review of Political Science, 15*, 9.1–9.21.

Holmén, H. (2010). *Snakes in paradise: NGOs and the aid industry in Africa.* Sterling, VA: Kumarian Press.

Holloway, R. (1998). NGOs—losing the moral high ground? *UN Chronicle, 35*, 93–94.

Hoogstraten, B. (2008). *The resistance fighters: The immense struggle of Holland during World War II.* Lanham, MD: Hamilton Books, Rowman & Littlefield.

Hopwood, B., Mellor, M., & O'Brien, G. (2005). Sustainable development: Mapping different approaches. *Sustainable Development, 13*, 38–52.

Horowitz, M. J. & Sorensen, J. E. (1978). *Evaluation of human service programs.* New York: Academic Press.

Howard, M. M. (2003). *The weakness of civil society in post-communist Europe.* Cambridge: Cambridge University Press.

Hrebenar, R. J. (1997). *Interest group politics in America*, 3rd edn. Armonk, NY: M. E. Sharpe.

Hudock, A. (1999). *NGOs and civil society: Democracy by proxy.* Cambridge: Polity.

Hudson, J. R. & Hudson, P. A. (2013). *Special interest society: How membership-based organizations shape America.* Lexington, MA: Lexington Books.

Humphreys, K. & Edwards, G. (Eds.) (2000). *Circles of recovery: Self-help organizations for addictions.* New York: Cambridge University Press.

Hunter, K. G., Wilson, L. A., & Brunk, G. G. (1991). Societal complexity and interest lobbying in the American states. *The Journal of Politics, 53*(02), 488–503.

Huntington, S. P. (1991). *The third wave: Democratization in the late twentieth century.* Norman, OK: University of Oklahoma Press.

Hutchinson, J. (1996). *Champions of charity: War and the rise of the Red Cross.* Boulder, CO: Westview Press.

Hybel, A. R. (2012). *The power of ideology: From the Roman empire to Al-Qaeda.* London: Routledge.

Hybels, B. (2004). *The volunteer revolution: Unleashing the power of everybody.* Grand Rapids, MI: Zondervan.

Imam, A. (2009). *Nonprofit organizations and the environmental policy outcomes: A systematic inquiry into the role of different types of nonprofits to influence the processes and outcomes of environmental policy.* Ann Arbor, MI: ProQuest, UMI Dissertations Publishing.

Inazu, J. D. (2012). *Freedom's refuge: The forgotten freedom of assembly.* New Haven, CT: Yale University Press.

Inglehart, R. (1997). *Modernization and postmodernization: Cultural, economic, and political change in 43 societies.* Princeton, NJ: Princeton University Press.

Inglehart, R., Basañez, M., Caterberg, G., Diez-Medrano, J., Moreno, A., Norris, P., Siemienska, R., & Zuasnabar, I. (Eds.) (2010). *Changing human beliefs and values, 1981–2007: Across-cultural sourcebook based on the world values surveys and European values studies.* Mexico City: Siglo XXI Editores.

Inglehart, R. & Welzel, C. (2005). *Modernization, cultural change, and democracy: The Human development sequence.* New York: Cambridge University Press.

Inkeles, A. & Smith, D. H. (1974). *Becoming modern.* Cambridge, MA: Harvard University Press. (Also Portuguese edition in Brazil, 1974, and two different Chinese editions, 1981 and 1992.)

Iriye, A. (2002). *Global community: The role of international organizations in the making of the contemporary world.* Berkeley, CA: University of California Press.

Jackson, R. (Ed.). (2016). *Routledge handbook of critical terrorism studies.* New York: Routledge.

Jackson, R., Jarvis, L. Gunning, J., & Breen-Smyth, M. (2016). *Terrorism: A critical introduction.* Basingstoke: Palgrave Macmillan.

Jacobson, S. & Colon, E. (2008). *After 9/11: America's war on terror (2001–).* New York: Hill and Wang.

Jasper, J. M. & Nelkin, D. (1992). *The animal rights crusade: The growth of a moral protest.* New York: Free Press.

Jedlicka, A. D. (1990). *Volunteerism and world development.* New York: Praeger.

Jeffreys-Jones, R. (2013). *The American left: Its impact on politics and society since 1900.* Edinburgh: Edinburgh University Press.

Jenkins, J. C. & Klandermans, B. (Eds.) (1995). *The politics of social protest.* Minneapolis, MN: University of Minnesota Press.

Johnson, A. W. & Earle, T. (1987). *The evolution of human societies: From foraging group to agrarian state.* Stanford, CA: Stanford University Press.

Johnson, E. W. (2008). Social movement size, organizational diversity and the making of federal law. *Social Forces, 86*(3), 967–993.

Johnstone, R. L. (1992). *Religion in society: A sociology of religion*, 4th edn. Englewood Cliffs, NJ: Prentice-Hall.

Joint, N., & Wallis, J. (2005). Information literacy and the role of national library and information associations. *Library Review, 54*(4), 213–217.

Jonas, G. (2007). *Freedom's sword: The NAACP and the struggle against racism in America, 1909–1969.* London: Routledge.

Jordan, L. & van Tuijl, P. (2007). *NGO accountability: Politics, principles and innovations.* London: Earthscan.

Jordan, R. S. (2001). *International organizations: A comparative approach to the management of cooperation*, 4th edn. Santa Barbara, CA: Praeger.

Josephus, Flavius (transl. W. Whiston). (1960). *The complete works of Josephus.* Grand Rapids, MI: Kregel Publications.

Juergensmeyer, M. (2003). *Terror in the mind of God: The global rise of religious violence.* 3rd edn. Berkeley, CA: University of California Press.

Juergensmeyer, M. (2009). *Global rebellion: Religious challenges to the secular state, from Christian militias to al Qaeda.* Berkeley, CA: University of California Press.

Juergensmeyer, M. (Ed.). (2011). *The Oxford handbook of global religions.* Oxford: Oxford University Press.

Juergensmeyer, M., Kitts, M., & Jerryson, M. (Eds.). (2015). *The Oxford handbook of religion and violence.* Oxford: Oxford University Press.

Kalyvas, S. N. (1996). *The rise of Christian democracy in Europe.* Ithaca, NY: Cornell University Press.

Kansal, A. (2012). *The evolution of gods: The Scientific origin of divinity and religions.* New Delhi: HarperCollins India.

Kanter, R. M. (1979). *The measurement of organizational effectiveness, productivity, performance and success: Issues and dilemmas in service and non-profit organizations,* vol. 8. New Haven, CT: Institution for Social and Policy Studies, Yale University.

Kanter, R. M. & Binkerhoff, D. (1981). Organizational performance: Recent developments in measurement. *Annual Review of Sociology, 7,* 321–349.

Katsourides, Y. (2016). *Radical left parties in government.* Basingstoke: Palgrave Macmillan.

Katz, A. H. (1993). *Self-help in America: A social movement perspective.* New York: Twayne.

Katz, A. H. & Bender, E. I. (1990). *Helping one another: Self-help groups in a changing world.* Oakland, CA: Third Party Publishing Co.

Katz, M. B. (1986). *In the shadow of the poorhouse: A social history of welfare in America.* New York: Basic Books.

Katz, R. S. & Crotty, W. J. (Eds.). (2005). *Handbook of party politics.* Thousand Oaks, CA: SAGE Publications.

Kaufman, J. A. (2002). *For the common good? American civic life in the golden age of fraternity.* New York: Oxford University Press.

Kearns, K. P. (2012). Accountability in the nonprofit sector. In Lester M. Salamon (Ed.), *The state of nonprofit America,* 2nd edn. (pp. 587–615). Washington, DC: Brookings Institution Press.

Kedward, R. (1991). *Occupied France: Collaboration and resistance 1940–1944.* New York: Wiley-Blackwell.

Keehley, P. & Abercrombie, N. (2008). *Benchmarking in the public and nonprofit sectors: Best practices for achieving performance breakthroughs,* 2nd edn. San Francisco, CA: Jossey-Bass.

Kennedy, D. J. (1995). Residential Associations as State Actors: Regulating the Impact of Gated Communities on Nonmembers. *The Yale Law Journal, 105*(3), 761–793.

Kennedy, D. (2004). *The dark sides of virtue: Reassessing international humanitarianism*. Princeton, NJ: Princeton University Press.

Kephart, W. M., & Zellner, W. W. (Eds.). (1994). *Extraordinary groups: An examination of unconventional lifestyles*, 5th edn. New York: St. Martin's Press.

Khandker, S. R., Koolwal, G. B., & Samad, H. A. (2010). *Handbook on impact evaluation: Quantitative methods and practices*. Washington, D.C.: World Bank Publications.

King, K. N. 2004. Neighborhood associations and urban decision making in Albuquerque. *Nonprofit Management and Leadership, 14*(4), 391–409.

Kirsch, A. D., Hume, K. M., & Jalandoni, N. T. (1999). *Giving and volunteering in the United States*. Washington, DC: INDEPENDENT SECTOR.

Kitcher, P. (2011). *The ethical project*. Cambridge, MA: Harvard University Press.

Klein, A. J. (2005). *Striking Back: The 1972 Munich Olympics Massacre and Israel's Deadly Response*. New York: Random House.

Klein, M. W. & Maxson, C. L. (2006). *Street gang patterns and policies*. New York: Oxford University Press.

Kloppenborg, J. S. & Wilson, S. G. (Eds.) (1996). *Voluntary associations in the Graeco-Roman world*. London: Routledge.

Kluver, H. (2009). Measuring interest group influence using quantitative text analysis. *European Union Politics, 10*(4), 535–549.

Knill, C. (2001). Private governance across multiple arenas: European interest association as interface actors. *Journal of European Public Policy, 8*(2), 227–246.

Knill, C., Debus, M., & Heichel, S. (2010). Do parties matter in internationalised policy areas? The impact of political parties on environmental policy outputs in 18 OECD countries, 1970–2000. *European Journal of Political Research, 49*(3), 301–336.

Knobel, D. T. (1996). *"America for the Americans": The nativist movement in the United States*. New York: Twayne.

Knoke, D. (1998). Who steals my purse steals trash—the structure of organizational influence reputation. *Journal of Theoretical Politics, 10*(4), 507–530.

Knoke, D. (1983). Organization sponsorship and influence reputation of social influence associations. *Social Forces, 61*(4), 11065–11087.

Knoke, D. (1986). Associations and interest groups. *Annual Review of Sociology, 12*, 1–21.

Knoke, D. (1988). Incentive in collective action organizations. *American Sociological Review, 53*, 311–329.

Knoke, D. (1990). *Organizing for collective action: The political economies of associations*. New York: Aldine de Gruyter.

Knoke, D. (1993). Trade associations in the American political economy. In David C. Hammack & Dennis R. Young (Eds.), *Nonprofit organizations in a market economy* (pp. 138–174). San Francisco, CA: Jossey-Bass.

Krause, E. A. (1996). *Death of the guilds: Professions, states, and the advance of capitalism, 1930 to the present*. New Haven, CT: Yale University Press.

Kroeber, A. L. (1948). *Anthropology*, rev. edn. New York: Harcourt, Brace & World.

Kuhn, T. S. (1962). *The structure of scientific revolutions*. Chicago, IL: University of Chicago Press.

Kupermus, T. (1999). Building democracy: An examination of religious associations in South Africa and Zimbabwe. *The Journal of Modern African Studies, 37*(4), 643–668.

Kurtz, L. F. (1997). *Self-help and support groups*. Thousand Oaks, CA: Sage.

Lam, Pui-Yan. (2002). As the flocks gather: How religion affects voluntary association participation. *Journal for the Scientific Study of Religion, 41*(3), 405–422.

Lam, Pui-Yan. (2006). Religion and civic culture: A cross-national study of voluntary association membership. *Journal for the Scientific Study of Religion, 45*(2), 177–193.

Lambert, J. M. (1891). *Two thousand years of gild life*. Hull: A. Brown & Sons.

Lambert, M. (1992). *Medieval heresy*, 2nd edn. Oxford: Blackwell Publishers.

Lampe, D. & Riis-Jorgensen, B. (2014). *Hitler's savage canary: A history of the Danish resistance in World War II*. New York: Arcade Publishing.

Lancourt, Joan E. (1979). *Confront or concede: The Alinsky citizen action organizations*. Lexington, MA: D. C. Heath.

Landau, S. (1993). *The guerrilla wars of Central America: Nicaragua, El Salvador and Guatemala*. London: Weidenfeld & Nicolson.

Lane, H. (1992). *The mask of benevolence: Disabling the deaf community*. New York: Knopf.

Lang, S. (2014). *NGOs, civil society, and the public sphere*. Cambridge: Cambridge University Press.

Langbein, L. I. (1986). Money and access: Some empirical evidence. *Journal of Politics, 48*(4), 1052–1062.

Lansford, T. (2015). *Political handbook of the world*. Washington, DC: CQ Press.

Laraña, E., Johnston, H., & Gusfield, J. R. (Eds.) (1994). *New social movements: From ideology to identity*. Philadelphia, PA: Temple University Press.

Laska, V. (1985). *Nazism, resistance, & holocaust in World War II*. Metuchen, NJ: Scarecrow Press.

Lauer, S. R. & Yan, M. C. (2013). Voluntary association involvement and immigrant network diversity. *International Migration, 51*(3), 133–150.

Laumann, E. O. & Knoke, D. (1987). *The organizational state: Social choice in national policy domains*. Madison, WI: University of Wisconsin Press.

Laumann, E. O., Knoke, D., & Yong-Hak Kim. (1985). An organizational approach to state policy formation: A comparative study of energy and health domains. *American Sociological Review, 50*(1), 1–19.

Laville, H. & Wilford, H. (2006). *The US government, citizen groups and the Cold War: The state–private network (Studies in Intelligence)*. London: Routledge.

Lecy, J. D., Schmitz, H. P., & Swedlund, H. (2012). Non-governmental and not-for-profit organizational effectiveness: A modern synthesis. *Voluntas, 23*, 434–457.

Leigh, R., Smith, D. H., Giesing, C., León, M. J., Haski-Leventhal, D., Lough, B. J., Mati, J. M., & Strassburg, S. 2011). *2011 state of the world's volunteerism report: Universal values for global well-being.* Bonn: United Nations Volunteers.

Leighley, J. E. (2012). *The Oxford handbook of American elections and political behavior.* Oxford: Oxford University Press.

Lele, S. M. (1991). Sustainable development: A critical review. *World Development, 19*(6), 607–621.

Leonard, G. (2002). *The invention of party politics.* Chapel Hill, NC: University of North Carolina Press.

Levine, D. H. (2012). *Politics, religion & society in Latin America.* Boulder, CO: Lynne Rienner Publishers.

Levitas, D. (2002). *The terrorist next door: The militia movement and the radical right.* New York: Thomas Dunne Books, St. Martin's Griffin.

Lewis, D. & Kanji, N. (2009). *Non-governmental organizations and development.* London: Routledge.

Lewis, J. R. (2008). *The Oxford handbook of new religious movements.* Oxford: Oxford University Press.

Lewis, J. R. (2011). *Violence and new religious movements.* Oxford: Oxford University Press.

Lijphart, A. (1977). *Democracy in plural societies: A comparative exploration.* New Haven, CT: Yale University Press.

Lijphart, A. (1999). *Patterns of democracy: Government forms and performance in thirty-six countries.* New Haven, CT: Yale University Press.

Liket, K. C. & Maas, K. (2013). Nonprofit organizational effectiveness: Analysis of best practices. *Nonprofit and Voluntary Sector Quarterly, 44*(2), 268–296.

Lipset, S. M. (1963). *The first new nation: The United States in historical and comparative perspective.* New York: Basic Books.

Littell, F. H. (1962). *From state church to pluralism.* Garden City, NY: Anchor Books.

Little, K. L. (1965). *West African urbanization: A study of voluntary associations.* Cambridge: Cambridge University Press.

Liu, H. (1998). Old linkages, new networks: The globalization of overseas Chinese voluntary associations and its implications. *The China Quarterly, 155*, 588–609.Lofland, J. F. (1996). *Social movement organizations.* New York: Aldine de Gruyter.

Lowery, D. & Brasher, H. (2004). *Organizational interests and American government.* New York: McGraw-Hill.

Lowie, R. H. (1970). *Primitive religion.* New York: Liveright/Norton.

Lowie, R. H. (1948). *Social organization.* New York: Rinehart.

Lowy, M. (1996). *The war of Gods: Religion and politics in Latin America.* New York: Verso.

Lubove, R. (1968). *The struggle for social security 1900–1935.* Cambridge, MA: Harvard University Press.

McAdam, D. (1982). *Political process and the development of black insurgency 1930–1970.* Chicago, IL: University of Chicago Press.

McBride, A. M., Sherraden, M. W., Benitez, C., & Johnson, E. (2004). Civic service worldwide: defining a field, building a knowledge base. *Nonprofit and Voluntary Sector Quarterly, 33,* 8S–21S.

McBride, A. M. & Sherraden, M. W. (Eds.) (2007). *Civic service worldwide: Impacts and inquiry.* Armonk, NY: M. E. Sharpe.

McCarthy, J. D. & Castelli, J. (2002). The necessity for studying organizational advocacy comparatively. In P. Flynn, & V. A. Hodgkinson, (Eds.), *Measuring the impact of the nonprofit sector* (pp. 103–121). New York: Kluwer Academic.

McCarthy, K. D. (1990). *Lady bountiful revisited: Women, philanthropy, and power.* New Brunswick, NJ: Rutgers University Press.

McCarthy, K. D. (1991). *Women's culture: American philanthropy and art, 1830–1930.* Chicago, IL: University of Chicago Press.

McCarthy, K. D., Hodgkinson, V. A., Sumariwalla, R. D., & Associates. (1992). *The nonprofit sector in the global community: Voices from many nations.* San Francisco, CA: Jossey-Bass.

McClellan, J. E. (1985). *Science reorganized: Scientific societies in the eighteenth century.* New York: Columbia University Press.

McDonough, F. (2003). *Hitler and the rise of the Nazi party.* New York: Pearson Longman.

McFarland, A. S. (1976). *Public interest lobbies: Decision making on energy.* Washington, DC: Enterprise Institute for Public Policy Research.

McKearney, T. (2011). *The provisional IRA.* London: Pluto Press.

McKenzie, E. (1994). *Privatopia: Homeowner associations and the rise of residential private government.* New Haven, CT: Yale University Press.

McLaverty, P. (2002). Civil society and democracy. *Contemporary Politics, 8*(4), 303–318.

Macleod, D. I. (1983). *Building character in the American boy: The Boy Scouts, YMCA, and their forerunners, 1870–1920.* Madison, WI: University of Wisconsin Press.

McWhirter, D. A. (1994). *Freedom of speech, press, and assembly.* Phoenix, AZ: Oryx.

Maier, P. (1992). *From resistance to revolution: Colonial radicals and the development of American opposition to Britain, 1765–1776.* New York: W. W. Norton.

Maisel, L. S. & Berry, J. (Eds.). (2010). *The Oxford handbook of American political parties and interest groups.* New York: Oxford University Press.

Malcolmson, P. & Malcolmson, R. (2013). *Women at the ready: The remarkable story of the Women's Voluntary Services on the home front.* London: Little, Brown.

Malefijt, A. De Waal. (1989). *Religion and culture: An introduction to anthropology of religion.* Long Grove, IL: Waveland Press.

March, J. G.,& Olsen, J. P. (1995). *Democratic governance.* New York: Free Press.

Markham, W. T. (2008). *Environmental organizations in modern Germany: Hard survivors in the twentieth century and beyond.* New York: Berghahn Books.

Marks, J. (1984). *Science and the making of the modern world*. Portsmouth, NH: Heinemann.

Martin, A. W. (2008). Resources for success: Social movements, strategic resource allocation, and union organizing outcomes. *Social Problems, 55*(4), 501–524.

Martin, D. (1981). *The struggle for Zimbabwe: The Chimurenga war*. New York: Monthly Review Press.

Mastny, V. (1971). *The Czechs under Nazi rule: The failure of national resistance, 1939–1942*. New York: Columbia University Press.

Mati, J., Wu, F., Edwards, B., El Taraboulsi, S. N., & Smith, D. H. (2016). Social movements and activist-protest volunteering. In D. H. Smith, R. A. Stebbins, and J. Grotz, (Eds.), *Palgrave Handbook of Volunteering, Civic Participation, and Nonprofit Associations* (pp. 516–538, Chapter 24). Basingstoke, UK: Palgrave Macmillan.

Mead, F. S. & Hill, S. S. (2001). *Handbook of denominations in the United States*. Nashville, TN: Abingdon Press.

Melton, J. G., Bevereley, J., Jones, C., & Nadell, P. S. (Eds.) (2009). *Melton's Encyclopedia of American Religions*, 8th ed. Detroit, MI: Gale.

Menzies, A. (2016). *History of religion*. Colorado Springs, CO: CreateSpace Independent Publishing Platform.

Merton, R. K. (1973). *The sociology of science*. Chicago, IL: University of Chicago Press.

Meyer, D. S. (2007). *The politics of protest: Social movements in America*. New York: Oxford University Press.

Meyer, D. S. (2014). *The politics of protest: Social movements in America*, 2nd edn. New York: Oxford University Press.

Meyer, D. S., Jenness, V., & Ingram, H. (Eds.) (2005). *Routing the opposition: Social movements, public policy, protest, and contention*. Minneapolis, MN: University of Minnesota Press.

Meyer, D. S. & Whittier, N. (1994). Social movement spillover. *Social Problems, 41*(2): 277–298.

Michels, R. (1962 [1915]). *Political parties: A sociological study of the oligarchical tendencies of modern democracy*. New York: Free Press.

Micklethwait, J. & Wooldridge, A. (2010). *God is back*. New York: Penguin.

Mihlar, F. (1999). *Unions and right to work laws: Global evidence of their impact on employment*. Vancouver: Frazer Institute.

Milkas, S. M. (1999). *Political parties and constitutional democracy*. Baltimore, MD: The Johns Hopkins University Press.

Milofsky, C. (1988). *Community organizations: Studies in resource mobilization and exchange*. New York: Oxford University Press.

Milofsky, C. (2008). *Smallville: Institutionalizing community in twenty-first century America*. Medford, MA: Tufts University Press.

Minkoff, D. C. (1995). *Organizing for equality: The evolution of women's and racial-ethnic organizations in America, 1955–1985.* Philadelphia, PA: Temple University Press.

Minkoff, D. C. (1997). Producing social capital: National social movements and civil society. *American Behavioral Scientist, 40*(5), 606–619.

Montgomery, Jr., R. L. (2012). *Why religions spread.* Warren, NJ: Cross Lines Publishing.

Moore, R. I. (1977 [1994]). *The origins of European dissent.* Toronto: University of Toronto Press.

More-Hollerweger, E., Bowman, W., Gavurova, B., & Kuvikova, H. (2016). Economics of associations and volunteering. In D. H. Smith, R. A. Stebbins, & J. Grotz (Eds.), *Palgrave handbook of volunteering, civic participation, and nonprofit associations* (pp. 1074–1090, Chapter 44). Basingstoke: Palgrave Macmillan.

Morgan, G. G. (2013). *Charitable incorporated organisations.* London: Directory of Social Change.

Morris, A. D. (1984). *The origins of the civil rights movement: Black communities organizing for change.* New York: Free Press.

Morrison, D. E. (Ed.) (1970). *Farmers' organizations and movements.* East Lansing, MI: Agricultural Experiment Station, Michigan State University, Research Bulletin 24.

Musick, M. A. & Wilson, J. (2008). *Volunteers: A social profile.* Bloomington, IN: Indiana University Press.

Napoleoni, L. (2005). *Terror incorporated: Tracing the dollars behind the terror networks.* New York: Seven Stories Press.

Nasr, V. (2007). *The Shia revival: How conflicts within Islam will shape the future.* New York: Norton.

Neem, J. N. (2008). *Creating a nation of joiners: Democracy and civil society in early national Massachusetts.* Cambridge, MA: Harvard University Press.

Ness, I. (Ed.) (2009). *The international encyclopedia of revolution and protest: 1500 to the present.* New York: Wiley-Blackwell.

Newberg, A., with Waldman, M. R. (2006). *Born to believe.* New York: Free Press.

Newcomb, T. M. & Wilson, E. K. (1966). *College peer groups.* Chicago, IL: Aldine.

Newcomer, K. E., Hatry, H. P., & Wholey, J. S. (2015). *Handbook of practical program evaluation*, 4th edn. San Francisco, CA: Jossey-Bass.

Nichols, G. (2017). Volunteering in community sports associations: A literature review. *Voluntaristics Review: Brill Research Perspectives, 2*(1), 1–75.

Nikkhah, H. A., & Zhairinia, M. (2011). Contribution of NGOs functions to empowerment of women in Shirfaz, Iran. *Life Science Journal, 8*(4), 490–496.

Nolan, P., & Lenski, G. (2006). *Human societies: An introduction to mascrosociology.* Boulder, CO: Paradigm Publishers.

Norris, P. (2002). *Democratic Phoenix: Reinventing political activism.* Cambridge: Cambridge University Press.

Novacek, C. (2012). *Border crossings: Coming of age in the Czech resistance.* Pittsburgh, PA: Dorrance Publishing, 1021 Press.

Obadare, E. (Ed.) (2014). *The handbook of civil society in Africa.* New York: Springer.

Oberg, P.O. & Svensson, T. (2012). Civil society and deliberative democracy: Have voluntary organisations faded from national public politics? *Scandinavian Political Studies, 35*(3), 246–271.

O'Brien, K. J. & Lianjiang Li. (2006). *Rightful resistance in rural China.* New York: Cambridge University Press.

Odendaal, A. (2013). *The founders: The origins of the ANC and the struggle for democracy in South Africa.* Lexington, KY: University Press of Kentucky.

Olzak, S. & Ryo, E. (2007). Organizational diversity, vitality and outcomes in the civil rights movement. *Social Forces, 85*(4), 1561–1591.

Olzak, S. & Soule, S. A. (2009). Cross-cutting influences of environmental protest and legislation. *Social Forces, 88*(1), 201–225.

O'Neill, M. (1989). *The third sector.* San Francisco, CA: Jossey-Bass.

O'Neill, M. (2002). *Nonprofit nation: A new look at the third America,* 2nd edn. San Francisco: Jossey-Bass.

Ornstein, M. (1963 [1913]). *The Role of scientific societies in the seventeenth century.* Hamden, CT: Archon Books.

Osborne, S. P. & Tricker, M. (1995). Researching Non-profit organisational effectiveness: A comment on Herman and Heimovics. *Voluntas, 6*(1), 85–92.

Pahl, G. & Jones, V. (2012). *Power to the people: How to organize, finance, and launch local energy projects.* White River Junction, VT: Chelsea Green Publishing.

Pais, Abraham. (1982). *'Subtle is the Lord ...': The science and life of Albert Einstein.* Oxford: Oxford University Press.

Panek, R. (2011). *The 4 percent universe: Dark matter, dark energy, and the race to discover the rest of reality.* Boston, MA: Houghton Mifflin Harcourt.

Parsons, T. (1966). *Societies: Evolutionary and comparative perspectives.* Englewood Cliffs, NJ: Prentice-Hall.

Pavone, C. & Levy, P. (2014). *A civil war: A history of the Italian resistance.* New York: Verso.

Pekkanen, R. (2006). *Japan's dual civil society: Members without advocates.* Stanford, CA: Stanford University Press.

Pelling, H. (1963). *A history of British trade unionism.* Baltimore, MD: Penguin.

Penna, R. M. (2011). *The nonprofit outcomes toolbox: A complete guide to program effectiveness, performance measurement and results.* New York: Wiley.

Penner, L. A. (2004). Volunteerism and social problems: Making things better or worse? *Journal of Social Issues, 60*(3), 645–666.

Perez, J. (2005). *The Spanish Inquisition: A history.* New Haven, CT: Yale University Press.

Perez-Diaz, V. (1993). *The return of civil society: The emergence of democratic Spain.* Cambridge, MA: Harvard University Press.

Perrow, C. P. (1961). The analysis of goals in complex organizations. *American Sociological Review, 26*(6), 854–866.

Pestoff, V. A. (1977). *Voluntary associations and Nordic party systems.* Stockholm: Stockholm University.

Pierce, J. L. (2006). *Greater Boston community theatre.* Mt. Pleasant, SC: Arcadia Publishing.

Pinker, S. (2012). *The better angels of our nature: Why violence has declined.* New York: Viking, Penguin.

Pinker, S. (2018). *Enlightenment now: The case for reason, science, humanism and progress.* New York: Viking.

Piven, F. F. (2006). *Challenging authority: How ordinary people change America.* Lanham, MD: Rowman & Littlefield.

Piven, F. F. & Cloward, R. A. (1979). *Poor people's movements: Why they succeed, how they fail.* New York: Vintage Books.

Points of Light Foundation. (2002). *Preventing a disaster within the disaster: The effective use and management of unaffiliated volunteers.* Washington, DC: Points of Light Foundation.

Poister, T. H., Aristigueta, M. P., & Hall, J. L. (2014). *Managing and measuring performance in public and nonprofit organizations*, 2nd edn. San Francisco, CA: Jossey-Bass.

Pol, E. & Ville, S. (2009). Social innovation: Buzz word or enduring term? *The Journal of Socio-Economics, 38*(6), 878–885.

Polk, W. R. (2008). *Violent politics: A history of insurgency, terrorism, and guerrilla war, from the American revolution to Iraq.* New York: Harper Perennial.

Polonsky, M. & Grau, S. L. (2011). Assessing the social impact of charitable organizations—four alternative approaches. *International Journal of Nonprofit and Voluntary Sector Marketing, 16*(2), 195–211.

Potok, A. (2002). *A matter of dignity: Changing the lives of the disabled.* New York: Bantam.

Powell, L., Williamson, J. B., & Branco, K. J. (1996). *The senior rights movement.* New York: Twayne.

Powell, W. W. & Clemens, E. S. (1998). *Private action and the public good.* New Haven, CT: Yale University Press.

Powell, W. W. & Steinberg, R. (Eds.) (2006). *The nonprofit sector: A research handbook*, 2nd edn. New Haven, CT: Yale University Press.

Pratt, H. J. (1974). Old age associations in national politics. *The Annals of the American Academy of Political and Social Science, 414*(1), 106–119.

Predelli, L. N. (2008). Political and cultural ethnic mobilisation: The role of immigrant associations in Norway. *Journal of Ethnic and Migration Studies, 34*(6), 935–954.

Preston, P. (2004). *Protestant political parties: A global survey.* London: Routledge.

Price, J. L. (1968). *Organizational effectiveness.* Homewood, IL: Irwin.

Prothero, S. (2011). *God is not one: The eight rival religions that run the world.* New York: Harper One.

Przeworski, A., Alvarez, M., Cheibub, J. A., & Limongi, F. (2000). *Democracy and development: Political institutions and well-being in the world, 1950–1990.* New York: Cambridge University Press.

Putnam, R. D. (1993). *Making democracy work: Civic traditions in modern Italy.* Princeton, NJ: Princeton University Press.

Putnam, R. D. (2000). *Bowling alone: The collapse and revival of American community.* New York: Simon & Schuster.

Pyenson, L. & Sheets-Pyenson, S. (2000). *Servants of nature: A history of scientific institutions, enterprises and sensibilities.* London: Fontana Press, HarperCollins.

Queen, C. (1996). *Engaged Buddhism: Buddhist liberation movements in Asia.* Albany, NY: State University of New York Press.

Rauch, J. (1995). *Demosclerosis: The silent killer of American government.* New York: Times Books.

Reagin, N. R. (1995). *A German women's movement: Class and gender in Hanover, 1880–1933.* Chapel Hill, NC: The University of North Carolina Press.

Redclift, M. (1987). *Sustainable development: Exploring the contradictions.* London: Routledge.

Redclift, M. (2005). Sustainable development (1987–2005): An oxymoron comes of age. *Sustainable Development, 13,* 212–227.

Redclift, M. & Springett, D. (Eds.) (2015). *Routledge international handbook of sustainable development.* London: Routledge.

Rehbock, P. F. (2001). Globalizing the history of science. *Journal of World History, 12*(1), 183–192.

Reichley, J. A. (2000). *The life of the parties: A history of American political parties.* Lanham, MD: Rowman & Littlefield.

Rennie, B. & Tite, P. L. (Eds.) (2008). *Region, terror, and violence: Religious studies perspectives.* New York: Routledge.

Renz, D. O. (Ed.) (2010). *The Jossey-Bass handbook of nonprofit leadership and management.* San Francisco, CA: Jossey-Bass.

Renz, D. O., & Herman, R. D. (Eds.). (2016). *The Jossey-Bass Handbook of Nonprofit Leadership and Management.* New York: Wiley.

Rheingold, H. (1994). *The virtual community.* New York: HarperCollins.

Rich, P. B. & Duyvesteyn, I. (2014). *The Routledge handbook of insurgency and counter-insurgency.* New York: Routledge.

Richardson, C. & Pisani, M. J. (2013). *The informal and underground economy of the south Texas border.* Austin, TX: University of Texas Press.

Rings, W. (1982). *Life with the enemy: Collaboration and resistance in Hitler's Europe, 1939–1945.* New York: Doubleday Books.

Rivers, G. (1986). *The war against the terrorists.* New York: Stein and Day.

Roberts, A. & Ash, T. G. (Eds.) (2009). *Civil resistance and power politics: The experience of non-violent action from Gandhi to the present.* New York: Oxford University Press.

Robertson, D. B. (Ed.). (1966). *Voluntary associations: A study of groups in free societies.* Richmond, VA: John Knox Press.

Robinson, J. P., Gershuny, J., Smith, D. H., Fisher, K., Lee, C. W., & Stebbins, R. A. 2016. Leisure and time use perspectives on volunteering. In D. H. Smith, R. A. Stebbins, and J. Grotz (Eds.) *Palgrave Handbook of Volunteering, Civic Participation, and Nonprofit Associations* (pp. 126–144, Chapter 4). Basingstoke: Palgrave Macmillan.

Rochester, C. (2013). *Rediscovering voluntary action: The beat of a different drum.* Basingstoke: Palgrave Macmillan.

Rochester, C., Paine, A. E., Howlett, S., with Zimmeck, M. (2010). *Volunteering and society in the 21st century.* Basingstoke: Palgrave Macmillan.

Rock, D. (1995). *Authoritarian Argentina: The nationalist movement, its history, and impact.* Berkeley, CA: University of California Press.

Rojek, C., Shaw, S. M., & Veal, A. J. (Eds.) (2006). *A handbook of leisure studies.* Basingstoke: Palgrave Macmillan.

Römer, T., & Geuss, R. (transl.) (2015). *The invention of God.* Cambridge, MA: Harvard University Press.

Rose, R., Mishler, W., & Haerpfer, C. (1998). *Democracy and its alternatives: Understanding post-communist societies.* Baltimore, MD: Johns Hopkins University Press.

Rosenblum, N. L. (2000). *Membership and morals.* Princeton, NJ: Princeton University Press.

Rosenthal, M. (1986). *Character factory: Baden-Powell's Boy Scouts and the imperatives of empire.* New York: Pantheon Books.

Ross, J. C. (1976). *An assembly of good fellows: Voluntary associations in history.* Westport, CT: Greenwood.

Rothschild, J. & Milofsky, C. (2006). The centrality of values, passions, and ethics in the nonprofit sector. *Nonprofit Management and Leadership, 17*(2), 137–143.

Rossi, P. H., Lipsey, M. W., & Freeman, H. E. (2003). *Evaluation: A systematic approach,* 7th edn. Thousand Oaks, CA: SAGE.

Rubin, B. M. (2009). *Guide to Islamist movements,* 2 vols. Armonk, NY: M. E. Sharpe.

Ruiter, S. & Dirk De Graaf, N. (2010). National religious context and volunteering more rigorous tests supporting the association. *American Sociological Review, 75*(1), 179–184.

Saitgalina, M., Ting Zhao, Stebbins, R. A., & Smith, D. H. (2016). Participation in trade and business associations. In D. H. Smith, R. A. Stebbins, & J. Grotz (Eds.), *Palgrave handbook of volunteering, civic participation, and nonprofit associations* (pp. 417–435, Chapter 19). Basingstoke: Palgrave Macmillan.

Salamon, L. M. (1994). The rise of the nonprofit sector. *Foreign Affairs, 73*(4), 109–122.

Salamon, L. M. (1995). *The Global associational revolution: The rise of the third sector on the world scene.* London: Demos.

Salamon, L. M. (Ed.) (2002). *The state of nonprofit America.* Washington, DC: Brookings Institution Press.

Salamon, L. M. (Ed.) (2012). *The state of nonprofit America*, 2nd edn. Washington, DC: Brookings Institution Press.

Salamon, L. M. & Anheier, H. K. (1992). In search of the non-profit Sector II: The problem of classification. *Voluntas 3*(Dec.), 267–309.

Salamon, L. M., Sokolowski, S. & Associates. (2004). *Global civic society: Dimensions of the nonprofit sector*, vol. 2. Bloomfield, CT: Kumarian.

Salamon, L. M., Wojchiech Sokolowski, S., & Haddock, M. A. (2011). Measuring the economic value of volunteer work globally: Concepts, estimates, and a roadmap to the future. *Annals of Public and Cooperative Economics, 82*, 217–252.

Sanborn, C. & Portocarrero, F. (2006). *Philanthropy and social change in Latin America.* Cambridge, MA: David Rockefeller Center for Latin American Studies, Harvard University.

Sanders, D. S. (1973). *Impact of reform movements on social policy change: The case of social insurance.* Fair Lawn, NJ: R. E. Burdick Publishers.

Saul, J. (2004). *Benchmarking for nonprofits: How to measure, manage, and improve performance.* Nashville, TN: Fieldstone Alliance.

Saurugger, S. (2008). Interest groups and democracy in the European Union. *West European Politics, 31*(6), 1274–1291.

Schain, M., Zolberg, A., & Hossey, P. (Eds.) (2002). *Shadows over Europe: The development and impact of the extreme right in Western Europe.* Basingstoke, UK: Palgrave Macmillan.

Scherer, R. (1972). The church as a formal voluntary organization. In D. H. Smith, R. D. Reddy, & B. R. Baldwin (Eds.), *Voluntary action research: 1972* (pp. 81–108). Lexington, MA: Lexington Books.

Scherr, A. (1989). *Freedom of protest, public order, and the law.* New York: Basil Blackwell.

Schlesinger, A. M. (1944). Biography of a nation of joiners. *American Historical Review, 50*(1), 1–25.

Schlozman, D. (2015). *When movements anchor parties.* Princeton, NJ: Princeton University Press.

Schlozman, K. L. & Tierney, J. (1986). *Organized interests and American democracy.* New York: Harper and Row.

Schlozman, K. L., Verba, S., & Brady, H. E. (2012). *The unheavenly chorus: Unequal political voice and the broken promise of American democracy*. Princeton, NJ: Princeton University Press.

Schmid, A. (2013). *The Routledge handbook of terrorism research*. New York: Routledge.

Schmidt, A. J. (1980). *Fraternal organizations*. Westport, CT: Greenwood Press.

Schoenbrun, D. 1980. *Solders of the night: The story of the French resistance*. New York: E. P. Dutton.

Schofer, E. (2003). The global institutionalization of geological science, 1800 to 1990. *American Sociological Review, 68*(5), 730–759.

Schofer, E. & Longhofer, W. (2011). The structural sources of association. *American Journal of Sociology, 117*(2), 539–585.

Scott, A. F. (1992). *Natural allies: Women's associations in American history*. Urbana, IL: University of Illinois Press.

Scott, J. C. (1985). *Weapons of the weak: Everyday forms of peasant resistance*. New Haven, CT: Yale University Press.

Scott, R. (1995). *Institutions and organizations*. Thousand Oaks, CA: SAGE.

Sehm-Patomaki, K. & Ulvila, M. (Eds.) (2007). *Global political parties*. London: Zed Books.

Seligman, M. E. P. (2012). *Flourish: A visionary new understanding of happiness and well-being*. New York: Simon and Schuster.

Selinger, C. (2000). *Stuff you don't learn in engineering school*. New York: Wiley-IEEE Press.

Service, E. R. (1975). *Origins of the state and civilization: The process of cultural evolution*. New York: Norton.

Seymour, P. (2008). *Dark matters: Unifying matter, dark matter, dark energy, and the universal grid*. Franklin Lakes, NJ: New Page Books.

Shafer, B. E. (Ed.) (1991). *Religion in ancient Egypt*. Ithaca, NY: Cornell University Press.

Shapiro, J. P. (1993). *No pity: People with disabilities forging a new civil rights movement*. New York: Times Books.

Sharp, G. & Paulson, J. (2005). *Waging nonviolent struggle*. Boston, MA: Porter Sargent.

Shock, K. (2015). *Civil resistance: Perspectives on nonviolent struggle*. Minneapolis, MN: University of Minnesota Press.

Shoham, A., Ruvio, A., Vigoda-Gadot, E., & Schwabsky, N. (2006). Market orientations in the nonprofit and voluntary sector: A meta-analysis of their relationships with organizational performance. *Nonprofit and Voluntary Sector Quarterly, 35*(3), 453–476.

Shultz, R. H. & Dew, A. J. (2006). *Insurgents, terrorists, and militias: The warriors of contemporary combat*. New York: Columbia University Press.

Silbey, J. H. (2002). *Martin Van Buren and the emergence of American popular politics*. Lanham, MD: Rowman & Littlefield.

Sills, D. L. (1957). *The volunteers: Means and ends in a national organization.* Glencoe, IL: Free Press.

Simmons, L. (1945). *The role of the aged in primitive society.* New Haven, CT: Yale University Press.

Simon, H. A. (1964). On the concept of organizational goal. *Administrative Science Quarterly, 9*(1), 1–22.

Simpson, R. L. & Gulley, W. H. (1962). Goals, environmental pressures, and organizational characteristics. *American Sociological Review, 27*(3), 344–351.

Sims, Patsy. (1996). *The klan,* 2nd edn. Lexington, KY: University Press of Kentucky.

Sirianni, C. & Friedland, L. (2001). *Civic innovation in America: Community empowerment, public policy, and the movement for civic renewal.* Berkeley, CA: University of California Press.

Skocpol, T. (1979). *States and social revolutions.* Cambridge: Cambridge University Press.

Skocpol, T. (1992). *Protecting soldiers and mothers: The political origins of social policy in the United States.* Cambridge, MA: Harvard University Press.

Skocpol, T. (2003). *Diminished democracy: From membership to management in American civic life.* Norman, OK: University of Oklahoma Press.

Skocpol, T. & Fiorina, M. P. (Eds.) (1999). *Civic engagement in American democracy.* Washington, DC: Brookings Institution.

Skocpol, T., Ganz, M., & Munson, Z. (2000). A nation of organizers: The institutional origins of civic voluntarism in the United States. *The American Political Science Review, 94*(3), 527–546.

Skrentny, J. D. (2004). *The minority rights revolution.* Cambridge, MA: Belknap Press.

Slezak, E. (2000). *The book group book: A thoughtful guide to forming and enjoying a stimulating book discussion group,* 3rd edn. Chicago, IL: Chicago Review Press.

Smillie, I. (2009). *Freedom from want: The remarkable success story of BRAC, the global grassroots organization that's winning the fight against poverty.* Sterling, VA: Kumarian Press.

Smith, C. & Freedman, A. (1972). *Voluntary associations: Perspectives on the literature.* Cambridge, MA: Harvard University Press.

Smith, D. H. (1967). A parsimonious definition of "group": Toward conceptual clarity and scientific utility. *Sociological Inquiry, 37,* 141–168.

Smith, D. H. (1972a). Modernization and the emergence of volunteer organizations. *International Journal of Comparative Sociology, 13,* 113–134.

Smith, D. H. (1972b). Organizational boundaries and organizational affiliates. *Sociology and Social Research, 56*(4), 494–512.

Smith, D. H. (1973a). *Latin American student activism.* Lexington, MA: Lexington Books, D. C. Heath and Company.

Smith, D. H. (Ed.) (1973b). *Voluntary action research: 1973.* Lexington, MA: Lexington Books.

Smith, D. H. (Ed.) (1974). *Voluntary action research: 1974. The nature of voluntary action around the world.* Lexington, MA: Lexington Books.

Smith, D. H. (1975). Voluntary action and voluntary groups. *Annual Review of Sociology, 1*, 247–70.

Smith, D. H. (1980). The impact of the voluntary sector on society. In Tracy Connors (Ed.), *The nonprofit organization handbook* (pp. 2.1–2.12). New York: McGraw-Hill. (Also included in 2nd edn, 1988.)

Smith, D. H. (1986). Outstanding local voluntary organizations in the 1960s: Their distinguishing characteristics. *Nonprofit and Voluntary Sector Quarterly, 15*(3), 24–35.

Smith, D. H. (1990). Voluntary inter-cultural exchange and understanding groups: The roots of success in U.S. sister city programs. *International Journal of Comparative Sociology, XXXI* (3&4), 177–192.

Smith, D. H. (1991). Four sectors or five? Retaining the member-benefit sector. *Nonprofit and Voluntary Sector Quarterly, 20*, 137–150.

Smith, D. H. (1992). National nonprofit, voluntary associations: Some parameters. *Nonprofit and Voluntary Sector Quarterly, 21*(1), 81–94.

Smith, D. H. (1993). Public benefit and member benefit nonprofit, voluntary groups. *Nonprofit and Voluntary Sector Quarterly, 22*(1), 53–68.

Smith, D. H. (1995). Democratic personality. In S. M. Lipset (Ed.), *The encyclopedia of democracy* (vol. 3) (pp. 941–943). Washington, DC: Congressional Quarterly Books.

Smith, D. H. (1997a). Grassroots associations are important: Some theory and a review of the impact literature. *Nonprofit and Voluntary Sector Quarterly, 26*(3), 269–306.

Smith, D. H. (1997b). The international history of grassroots associations. *International Journal of Comparative Sociology, 38*(3–4), 189–216.

Smith, D. H. (1997c). The rest of the nonprofit sector: Grassroots associations as the dark matter ignored in prevailing "flat-earth" maps of the sector. *Nonprofit and Voluntary Sector Quarterly, 26*, 114–131.

Smith, D. H. (1999a). Researching volunteer associations and other nonprofits: An emergent interdisciplinary field and possible new discipline. *The American Sociologist, 30* (4), 5–35.

Smith, D. H. (1999b). The effective grassroots association, I: Organizational factors that produce internal impact. *Nonprofit Management & Leadership, 9*(4), 443–456.

Smith, D. H. (1999c). The effective grassroots association, II: Organizational factors that produce external impact. *Nonprofit Management & Leadership, 10*(1), 103–116.

Smith, D. H. (2000). *Grassroots associations.* Thousand Oaks, CA: Sage Publications.

Smith, D. H. (2001). The impact of the voluntary sector on society. In J. Steven Ott (Ed.), *The nature of the nonprofit sector* (pp. 79–87). Boulder, CO: Westview Press.

Smith, D. H. (2003). "A history of ARNOVA" *Nonprofit and Voluntary Sector Quarterly*, *32*(3), 458–472.

Smith, D. H. (2004). Grassroots association. In D. Burlingame (Ed.), *Philanthropy in America: A comprehensive historical encyclopedia*, vol. I (pp. 211–215). Santa Barbara, CA: ABC-CLIO.

Smith, D. H. (2008a). Accepting and understanding the "dark side" of the nonprofit sector: One key part of building a healthier civil society. Paper presented at the Annual Conference of the Association for Research on Nonprofit Organisations and Voluntary Action. Philadelphia, PA, November 20–22.

Smith, D. H. (2008b). Comparative study of fundamentally deviant nonprofit groups and their role in global civil society and democratic cultures as a new frontier for third sector research: Evidence for prevalence of the false "angelic" nonprofit groups flat-earth paradigm. Paper presented at the Biennial Conference of The International Society for Third Sector Research, Barcelona, July 9–12.

Smith, D. H. (2010a). Grassroots associations. In H. K. Anheier, S. Toepler, & R. List (Eds.), *International Encyclopedia of Civil Society* (pp. 804–810). New York: Springer.

Smith, D H. (2010b). Membership and membership associations. In H. K. Anheier, S. Toepler, & R. List (Eds.), *International encyclopedia of civil society* (pp. 982–990). New York: Springer.

Smith, D. H. (2013). Growth of research associations and journals in the emerging discipline of altruistics. *Nonprofit and Voluntary Sector Quarterly, 42*(4), 638–656.

Smith, D. H. (2014a). An interdisciplinary theory of individual volunteering and why so few researchers have tested it. *Civil Society in Russia and Beyond* (English translation of journal name, published in Russian), *5*(2), 35–42.

Smith, D. H. (2014b). S-theory: Explaining individual behavior. (In Russian, in the Russian-language journal) *Институт языкознания РАН* [*Journal of Psycholinguistics*], *22*(4), 139–157.

Smith, D. H. (2014c). The current state of civil society and volunteering in the world, the USA, and China. *China Nonprofit Review* (English edition), *6*(1), 137–150.

Smith, D. H. (2015a). A theory of everyone: S-theory as a comprehensive, interdisciplinary, consilient, quantitative new paradigm for explaining human individual behavior applied to explaining volunteering in Russia. Paper presented at Annual Conference of ARNOVA, Chicago, IL, November 19–21.

Smith, D. H. (2015b). Voluntary associations, sociology of. In J. D. Wright (Editor-in-chief), *International encyclopedia of the social & behavioral sciences*, 2nd edn, vol. 25 (pp. 252–260). Oxford: Elsevier.

Smith, D. H. (2015c.) Voluntary organizations. In J. D. Wright (Editor-in-chief), *International encyclopedia of the social & behavioral sciences*, 2nd edn, vol. 25 (pp. 261–267). Oxford: Elsevier.

Smith, D. H. (2016a). A survey of voluntaristics: Research on the growth of the global, interdisciplinary, socio-behavioral science field and emergent inter-discipline. *Voluntaristics Review: Brill Research Perspectives, 1*(2), 1–81.

Smith, D. H. (2016b). Volunteering impacts on volunteers: Immediate positive emotional-cognitive effects and longer-term happiness/well-being effects. In D. H. Smith, R. A. Stebbins, & J. Grotz (Eds.), *Palgrave handbook of volunteering, civic participation, and nonprofit associations* (pp. 1312–1330, Chapter 53). Basingstoke: Palgrave Macmillan.

Smith, D. H. (2017a). Differences between nonprofit agencies and membership associations. In A. Farazmand (Ed.), *Global encyclopedia of public administration, public policy, and governance*. New York: Springer.

Smith, D. H. (2017b). Misconduct and deviance in and by nonprofit organizations. In A. Farazmand (Ed.), *Global encyclopedia of public administration, public policy, and governance*. New York: Springer.

Smith, D. H. (2017c). Sociological study of nonprofit organizations. In A. Farazmand (Ed.), *Global encyclopedia of public administration, public policy, and governance*. New York: Springer.

Smith, D. H. (2017d). The Global, Historical and Contemporary Impacts of Voluntary Membership Associations on Human Societies. *Voluntaristics Review: Brill Research Perspectives, 2*(5–6), 1–125.

Smith, D. H. (2018a forthcoming). *A survey of deviant voluntary associations: Seeking 'method in their madness' by developing an empirically supported theory of the dark side of the voluntary nonprofit sector.* Leiden and Boston, MA: Brill.

Smith, D. H. (2018b forthcoming). *Nonprofits daring to be different: Changing the world through collective deviant voluntary action.* Bradenton, FL: David Horton Smith International.

Smith, D. H. (2018c forthcoming). Democracy in America 180 years after De Tocqueville: Old and new types of citizen participation in local government. Chestnut Hill, MA: Department of Sociology, Boston College, unpublished paper submitted for editorial review.

Smith, D. H. (2018d in press). Four global associational revolutions: Explaining their causes and setting straight the historical record. *Civil Society in Russia and Abroad, 7*.

Smith, D. H. (2019 forthcoming). *S-theory (synanthrometrics) as a theory of everyone: A proposed new standard human science model of behavior.* Bradenton, FL: David Horton Smith International.

Smith, D. H., Baldwin, B. R., & Chittick, W. O. (1980). U.S. transnational voluntary organizations and international development. *International Journal of Comparative Sociology, 21*(3–4), 10–25.

Smith, D. H., Conley, W., Silver, H., Marsh, B., Orme, C., & Glasker, D. (1974). *Voluntary transnational cultural exchange organizations of the U. S.: A selected list.* Washington, DC: Center for a Voluntary Society.

Smith, D. H., with Dixon, J. (1973). The voluntary society. In Edward C. Bursk (Ed.), *Challenge to leadership* (pp. 202–227). New York: Free Press.

Smith, D. H. & Elkin, F. (1980). Volunteers, voluntary organizations, and development: An introduction. *International Journal of Comparative Sociology, XXI* (3–4), 1–9.

Smith, D. H. & Elkin, F. (Eds.) (1981). *Volunteers, voluntary associations, and development*. Leiden: E. J. Brill.

Smith, D. H., with Eng, S. & and Albertson, K. (2016). The darker side of philanthropy: How self-interest and incompetence can overcome a love of mankind and serving the public interest. In T. Jung, S. Phillips, & J. Harrow (Eds.), *The Routledge companion to philanthropy* (pp. 273–286, Chapter 18). London: Routledge.

Smith, D. H., Moldavanova, A. V., & Krasynska, S. (Eds.) (2018 in press). *The nonprofit sector in Eastern Europe, Russia, and Central Asia: Civil society advances and challenges*. Leiden, and Boston, MA: Brill.

Smith, D. H., Never, B., Mohan, J., Prouteau, L., & Torpe, L. (2016a). Prevalence rates of associations across territories. In D. H. Smith, R. A. Stebbins, & J. Grotz (Eds.), *Palgrave handbook of volunteering, civic participation, and nonprofit associations* (pp. 1210–1238, Chapter 50). Basingstoke: Palgrave Macmillan.

Smith, D. H., Never, B. Abu-Rumman, S., Afaq, A. K. Bethmann, S., Gavelin, K., Heitman, J. H., Jaishi, T., Kutty, A. D., Mwathi Mati, J., Paturyan, Y. J., Petrov, R., Pospíšilová, T., Svedberg, L., & Torpe, L. (2016b). Scope and trends of volunteering and associations. In D. H. Smith, R. A. Stebbins, & J. Grotz (Eds.), *Palgrave handbook of volunteering, civic participation, and nonprofit associations* (pp. 1241–1283, Chapter 51). Basingstoke: Palgrave Macmillan.

Smith, D. H., Pospíšilová, T., & Wu, F. (2016). National and other supra-local associations: Meso-associations. In D. H. Smith, R. A. Stebbins, & J. Grotz (Eds.), *Palgrave handbook of volunteering, civic participation, and nonprofit associations* (pp. 836–873, Chapter 33). Basingstoke: Palgrave Macmillan.

Smith, D. H., Reddy, R. D., & Baldwin, B. R. (Eds.) (1972). *Voluntary action research: 1972*. Lexington, MA: Lexington Books, D. C. Heath.

Smith, D. H. & Shen, C. (1996). Factors characterizing the most effective nonprofits managed by volunteers. *Nonprofit Management and Leadership, 6*(3), 271–289.

Smith, D. H. & Shen, C. (2002). The roots of civil society: A model of voluntary association prevalence applied to data on larger contemporary nations. *International Journal of Comparative Sociology, 42*(2), 93–133.

Smith, D. H., Stebbins, R. A., & Dover, M. (2006). *A dictionary of nonprofit terms and concepts.* Bloomington, IN: Indiana University Press.

Smith, D. H., Stebbins, R. A., & J. Grotz (Eds.) (2016). *Palgrave handbook of volunteering, civic participation, and nonprofit associations*. Basingstoke: Palgrave Macmillan.

Smith, D. H., with Stebbins, R. A., Grotz, J., Kumar, P., Nga, J., & van Puyvelde, S. (2016). Typologies of associations and volunteering. In D. H. Smith, R. A. Stebbins, & J. Grotz

(Eds.), *Palgrave handbook of volunteering, civic participation, and nonprofit associations* (pp. 90–125, Chapter 3). Basingstoke: Palgrave Macmillan.

Smith, D. H. & Sundblom, D. (2014). Growth of research-information centers, university departments, and schools/colleges in the emerging discipline of voluntaristics-altruistics. Paper presented at the Annual Conference of ARNOVA, Denver, CO, November 21–23.

Smith, D. H. & van Puyvelde, S. (2016a). S-Theory as a comprehensive, interdisciplinary explanation of volunteering and pro-social behavior. In D. H. Smith, R. A. Stebbins, & J. Grotz (Eds.), *Palgrave handbook of volunteering, civic participation, and nonprofit associations* (pp. 752–803, Chapter 31). Basingstoke, UK: Palgrave Macmillan.

Smith, D. H., with van Puyvelde. S. (2016b). Theories of associations and volunteering. In D.H. Smith, R. A. Stebbins, and J. Grotz (Eds.), *Palgrave Handbook of Volunteering, Civic Participation, and Nonprofit Associations* (pp. 59–89, Chapter 2). Basingstoke, UK: Palgrave Macmillan.

Smith, D. H. and Van Til, J., with Bernfeld, D., Pestoff, V., & Zeldin, D. (Eds.) (1983). *International perspectives on voluntary action research.* Lanham, MD: University Press of America.

Smith, D. H., Verhagen, F., Baldwin, B. R., & Chittick, W. (1978). *Role of U.S. NGOs in international development co-operation.* Paper No. 9, Series on Non-Governmental Organizations [NGOs] in International Co-Operation for Development, Berhanykun Andemicael (Ed.). New York: UNITAR, United Nations.

Smith, D. H., with Ting Zhao. (2016). Review and assessment of China's nonprofit sector after Mao: Emerging civil society? *Voluntaristics Review: Brill Research Perspectives, 1*(5), 1–67.

Smith, J. (2008). *Social movements for global democracy.* Baltimore, MD: Johns Hopkins University Press.

Smith, J. D. (Ed.) (1993). *Volunteering in Europe: Opportunities and challenges for the 90s.* London: The Volunteer Centre.

Smith, P. C. & Richmond, K. A. (2007). Call for greater accountability within the U.S. nonprofit sector. *Academy of Accounting and Financial Studies Journal, 11*(2), 75–88.

Smith, R. A. (1995). Interest group influence in the U.S. Congress. *Legislative Studies Quarterly, XX* (1), 89–139.

Smock, K. (2004). *Democracy in action: Community organizing and urban change.* New York: Columbia University.

Snelling, J. (1998). *The Buddhist handbook.* Rochester, VT: Inner Traditions International.

Snow, D. A., Della Porta, D., Klandermans, B., & McAdam, D. (Eds.) (2013). *The Wiley-Blackwell encyclopedia of social and political movements*, 3 vols. New York: Wiley-Blackwell.

HISTORICAL IMPACTS OF VOLUNTARY ASSOCIATIONS

Snow, D. A., Soule, S. A., & Kriesi, H. (Eds.) (2004). *The Blackwell companion to social movements*. Malden, MA: Blackwell Publishing.

Snyder, G. (2011). *Silence: The impending threat to the charitable sector*. Bloomington, IN: Xlibris.

Soteri-Proctor, A., Smith, D. H., Pospíšilová, T., Roka, K., & Yu, P. (2016). Local or grass-roots associations: Micro-associations. In D. H. Smith, R. A. Stebbins, & J. Grotz (Eds.), *Palgrave handbook of volunteering, civic participation, and nonprofit associations* (pp. 807–835; Chapter 32). Basingstoke: Palgrave Macmillan.

Soule, S. A. & Olzak, S. (2004). When do movements matter? The politics of contingency and the equal rights amendment. *American Sociological Review, 69*(4), 473–497.

Southers, E. (2013). *Homegrown violent extremism*. New York: Routledge.

Sowa, J. E., Coleman Selden, S., & Sandfort, J. R. (2004). No longer unmeasurable? A multidimensional integrated model of nonprofit organizational effectiveness. *Nonprofit and Voluntary Sector Quarterly, 33*(4), 711–728.

Spergel, I. A. (1995). *The youth gang problem: A community approach*. New York: Oxford University Press.

Spillman, L. (2012). *Solidarity in strategy: Making business meaningful in American trade associations*. Chicago, IL: University of Chicago Press.

Spray, S. L. (1976). *Organizational effectiveness*. Kent, OH: Kent State University Press.

Springer, D. R. (2009). *Islamic radicalism and global Jihad*. Washington, DC: Georgetown University Press.

Sproul, R. C. & Saleeb, A. (2003). *The dark side of Islam*. Wheaton, IL: Crossway Books, Good News Publishers.

Stahura, B. (1999). *Hoosier farmers—Indiana farm bureau*. Nashville, TN: Turner Publishing.

Stark, R. (1997). *The rise of Christianity*. San Francisco, CA: HarperSanFrancisco.

Stark, R. (2012). *The triumph of Christianity*. New York: HarperOne.

Stebbins, R. A. (2002). *The organizational basis of leisure participation: A motivation exploration*. State College, PA: Venture.

Stern, J. (2003). *Terror in the name of God: Why religious militants kill*. New York: Harper Perennial.

Stern, K. (2013). *With charity for all*. New York: Doubleday.

Stern, K. S. (1996). *A force upon the plain: The American militia movement and the politics of hate*. New York: Simon & Schuster.

Storer, N. W. (1966). *The social system of science*. New York: Holt, Rinehart, & Winston.

Stout, J. (2010). *Blessed are the organized: Grassroots democracy in America*. Princeton, NJ: Princeton University Press.

Straus, S. (2015). *Making and unmaking nations: War, leadership, and genocide in modern Africa*. Ithaca, NY: Cornell University Press.

Strom, K. (1990). A behavioral theory of competitive political parties. *American Journal of Political Science, 34*(2), 565–598.

Stutje, J. W. (2012). *Charismatic leadership and social movements*. New York: Berghahn Books.

Sundararajan, A. (2017). *The sharing economy: The end of employment and the rise of crowd-based capitalism*. Cambridge, MA: MIT Press.

Tannenbaum, A. S. (1961). Control and effectiveness in a voluntary organization. *American Journal of Sociology, 67*(1), 33–46.

Tarrow, S. (1998). *Power in movement: Social movements and contentious politics*. 2nd edn. Cambridge: Cambridge University Press.

Tarrow, S. (2006). *The new transnational activism*. New York: Cambridge University Press.

Tassie, B. & Murray, V. (1994). Evaluating the effectiveness of nonprofit organizations. In Robert D. Herman & Associates (Eds.), *The Jossey-Bass handbook of nonprofit leadership management* (pp. 303–324). San Francisco, CA: Jossey-Bass Publishers.

Taylor, C. (2007). *A secular age*. Cambridge, MA: Belknap Press, Harvard University Press.

Teorell, J. (2010). *Determinants of democratization: Explaining regime change in the world, 1972–2006*. New York: Cambridge University Press.

The Young Foundation. (2012). *Social innovation overview—Part I: Defining social innovation*. A deliverable to the project "The theoretical, empirical and policy foundations for building social innovation in Europe." Brussels: DG Research.

Thomas, C. S. (Ed.) (2004). *Research guide to U. S. and international interest groups*. Westport, CT: Praeger.

Thomas, S. M. (2005). *The global resurgence of religion and the transformation of international relations*. Basingstoke: Palgrave Macmillan.

Thomas-Slayter, B. P. (1985). *Politics, participation, and poverty: Development through self-help in Kenya*. Boulder, CO: Westview Press.

Thomson, J. A. & Aukofer, C. (2011). *Why we believe in gods: A concise guide to the science of faith*. Charlottesville, VA: Pitchstone Publishing.

Thompson, J. D. & McEwen, W. J. (1958). Organizational goals and environment: Goal-setting as an interaction process. *American Sociological Review, 23*, 23–31.

Thornberry, T. P., Krohn, M. D., Lizotte, A. J., Smith, C. A., & Tobin, K. (2003). *Gangs and delinquency in developmental perspective*. Cambridge: Cambridge University Press.

Tilly, C. (1993). *European revolutions, 1492–1992*. Oxford: Blackwell.

Tilly, C. (2004). *Social movements, 1768–2004*. Boulder, CO: Paradigm Publishers.

Tilly, C. (2007). *Democracy*. New York: Cambridge University Press.

Toft, M. D., Philpott, D., & Shah, T. (2011). *God's century: Resurgent religion and global politics*. New York: W. W. Norton.

Tucker, R. K. (1991). *The dragon and the cross: The rise and fall of the Ku Klux Klan in middle America.* Hamden, CT: Archon Books, Shoe String Press.

Turner, J. H. (2003). *Human institutions: A theory of societal evolution.* Lanham, MD: Rowman & Littlefield.

Uba, K. (2009). The contextual dependence of movement outcomes: A simplified meta-analysis. *Mobilization, 14*(4), 433–448.

Unger, B. & Van Waarden, F. (1999). Interest associations and economic growth: A critique of Mancur Olson's rise and decline of nations. *Review of International Political Economy, 6*(4), 425–467.

Vallory, E. (2012). *World scouting: Educating for global citizenship.* New York: Palgrave Macmillan.

Van Buren, M. (2015). *Inquiry into the origin and course of political parties in the United States.* Colorado Springs, CO: CreateSpace Independent Publishing Platform.

Van Deth, J. W. (Ed.) (1997). *Private groups and public life: Social participation, voluntary associations, and political involvement in representative democracies.* London: Routledge.

Vanhanen, T. (2003). *Measures of Democracy 1810–2002.* Tampere: University of Tampere, Finnish Social Science Data Archive.

Vaughn, J. (2003). *Disabled rights: American disability policy and the fight for equality.* Washington, D.C: Georgetown University Press.

Victor, J. N. (2002). Interest groups *do* influence Congress (but it's not about money). Paper presented at the 2002 Midwest Political Science Association Meetings, Chicago, IL (pp. 1–36).

Vigil, J. D. (2002). *A rainbow of gangs: Street cultures in the mega-city.* Austin, TX: University of Texas Press.

Vile, J. R. (2012). *The writing and ratification of the U. S. constitution.* Lanham, MD: Rowman & Littlefield.

Wade, N. (2009). *The faith instinct: How religion evolved and why it endures.* New York: Penguin.

Wagner, D. (2000). *What's love got to do with it? A critical look at American charity.* New York: The New Press.

Wake-Walker, E. (2008). *The lifeboats story: In association with the RNLI.* Stroud: Sutton Publishing.

Wald, K. D. & Calhoun-Brown, A. (2006). *Religion and politics in the United States,* 5th edn. Lanham, MD: Rowman & Littlefield.

Walker, J. L., Jr. (1983). The origins and maintenance of interest groups in America. *American Political Science Review, 77*(2): 390–406.

Walker, J. L., Jr. (1991). *Mobilizing interest groups in America: Patrons, professions, and social movements.* Ann Arbor, MI: University of Michigan Press.

Waltman, M. (2014). *Hate on the right: Right-wing political groups and hate speech*. Bern, Switzerland: Peter Lang Inc. International Academic Publishers.

Waltzing, J. P. (1895). *Etude Historique sur les Corporations Professionelles chez les Romains depuis les Origines jusquà la Chute de l'Empire d'Occident* [*History of Roman occupational organizations from their origins to the fall of the empire in the west*], 4 vols. Louvain: Paters.

Walzer, M. (1983). *Spheres of justice: A defense of pluralism and equality*. New York: Basic Books.

Wang, Ming (Ed.) (2011). *Emerging civil society in China, 1978–2008*. Leiden: Brill.

Ware, A. (2001). *Political parties and party systems*. New York: Oxford University Press.

Warin, P. (2002). The role of nonprofit associations in combating social exclusion in France. *Public Administration and Development, 22*(1), 73–82.

Warner, W. L. (Ed.) (1967). *Emergent American society: Large-scale organizations*. New Haven, CT: Yale University Press.

Warren, M. E. (2001). *Democracy and association*. Princeton, NJ: Princeton University Press.

Warren, M. R. (2001). *Dry bones rattling: Community building to revitalize democracy*. Princeton, NJ: Princeton University Press.

Warrick, J. (2016). *Black flags: The rise of ISIS*. New York: Anchor.

Wattenberg, M. P. (2009). *The decline of American political parties, 1952–1996*. Cambridge, MA: Harvard University Press.

Webster, H. (1908). *Primitive secret societies*. New York: Macmillan.

Weisberg, D. B. (1967). *Guild structure and political allegiance in early Achaemenid Mesopotamia*. New Haven, CT: Yale University Press.

Weisbrod, B. A. (1977). *The voluntary nonprofit sector: An economic analysis*. Lexington, MA: D. C. Heath.

Weisbrod, B. A. (1988). *The nonprofit economy*. Cambridge, MA: Harvard University Press.

Weisbrod, B. A. (1992). Tax policy toward nonprofit organizations: A Ten country survey. In K. D. McCarthy, V. A. Hodgkinson, & R. A. Sumariwalla (Eds.), *The nonprofit sector in the global community: Voices from many nations* (pp. 29–50). San Francisco, CA: Jossey-Bass.

Weisbrod, B. A. (Ed.) (1998). *To profit or not to profit: The commercial transformation of the nonprofit sector.* New York: Cambridge University Press.

Wesley, E. B. (1957). *NEA: The first hundred years: The Building of the teaching profession.* New York: Harper.

White, A. D. ([1896] 1993). *A history of the warfare of science with theology in Christendom*, 2 vols. Amherst, NY: Prometheus Books.

White, D. (2004). The voluntary sector, community sector and social economy in Canada: Why one is not the other. *Nonprofit and Civil Society Studies* (pp. 117–141). New York: Springer Nature.

White, D. (2006). *Charity on trial.* Fort Lee, NJ: Barricade Books.

Wholey, J. S., Hatry, H. P., & Newcomer, K. E. (2010). *Handbook of practical program evaluation,* 3RD ed. San Francisco, CA: Jossey-Bass.

Wilcox, C. & Robinson, C. (2010). *Onward Christian soldiers? The religious right in American politics.* Boulder, CO: Westview Press.

Willetts, P. (2011). *Non-governmental organisations in world politics.* London: Routledge.

Williams, D. K. (2012). *God's own party: The making of the Christian right.* Oxford: Oxford University Press.

Williams, M. (2006). *The impact of radical right-wing parties in West European democracies.* Basingstoke: Palgrave Macmillan.

Wilson, E. O. (2004 [1978]). *On human nature,* 2nd edn. Cambridge, MA: Harvard University Press.

Wilson, J., Joonmo Son, Smith, D. H., & Grotz, J. (2016). Longer-term volunteering impacts on volunteers and association members/participants. In D. H. Smith, R. A. Stebbins, & J. Grotz (Eds.), *Palgrave handbook of volunteering, civic participation, and nonprofit associations* (pp. 1284–1311, Chapter 52). Basingstoke: Palgrave Macmillan.

Wilts, A. & Meyer, M. (2005). Small firm membership in national trade associations. *Journal of Public Affairs, 5*(2), 176–185.

Wolfenden Committee. 1978. *The future of voluntary organisations: Report of the Wolfenden Committee.* London: Croom Helm.

Woliver, L. R. (1993). *From outrage to action: The politics of grass-roots dissent.* Urbana, IL: University of Illinois Press.

Woods, L. (2008). *Understanding world religions: A Bible-based review of 50 faiths.* Uhrichsville, OH: Barbour Publishing.

Wright, L. (2006). *The looming tower: Al-Qaeda and the road to 9/11.* New York: Knopf.

Wright, L. (2017). *The terror years: From al-Qaeda to the Islamic state.* New York: Vintage.

Wright, R. (2009). *The evolution of God.* Boston, MA: Little, Brown.

Wuthnow, R. (1994). *Sharing the journey: Support groups and America's new quest for community.* New York: Free Press.

Yackee, J. W. & Yackee, S. W. (2006). A bias toward business? Assessing interest group influence on the U.S. bureaucracy. *Journal of Politics, 68*(1), 128–139.

Young, K. (2016). *Sociology of sport: A global subdiscipline in review.* Bingley: Emerald Group Publishing.

Zack, G. M. (2003). *Fraud and abuse in nonprofit organizations: A guide to prevention and detection.* Hoboken, NJ: Wiley.

Zerubavel, E. T. (1992). *Terra cognita: The mental discovery of America.* New Brunswick, NJ: Rutgers University Press.

Zheng, Y. (2010). *The Chinese communist party as organizational emperor.* London: Routledge.